"Who Told You That You Were Naked?"

Genesis 3:11

(Greek meaning "in the beginning")

Copyright © 2018

By Dorothy

All rights reserved

Never do things half-way; it's a waste of time, cause you have to go back to redo it and get it right.

Table of Contents

TABLE OF CONTENTS 5

INTRODUCTION 7

WHO TOLD YOU THAT YOU WERE GAY? 11

WHO TOLD YOU THAT YOU WERE A PROSTITUTE? 35

WHO TOLD YOU THAT YOU WERE AN ORPHAN? (THE SPIRIT OF ABANDONMENT) 69

WHO TOLD YOU THAT YOU WERE POOR? (POOR MENTALITY) 85

WHO TOLD YOU TO COMMIT SUICIDE? 103

WHO TOLD YOU THAT YOU WERE A DOORMAT? (PHYSICAL AND MENTAL ABUSE) 119

WHO TOLD YOU THAT YOU WERE A THIEF? 139

WHO TOLD YOU THAT YOU WERE A LIAR? 151

WHO TOLD YOU THAT YOU WERE A THUG? 163

MY PROCESS 177

IN CLOSING 191

ACKNOWLEDGEMENTS 195

INTRODUCTION

We are now in the times where everyone does whatever they want to do. We have no regard for other people and their feelings. According to Genesis 3, God gave specific instructions of what we can and can't do. But, of course, we must have everything our flesh and appetites desire, even if it belongs to someone else. It's sad but true.

It is said that the acronym for the word Bible stands for "Basic Instructions Before Leaving Earth." What happened to having morals and abiding by God's instructions? If we follow instructions, the Bible explains how we ought to live, how to love, and what the consequences of our actions are.

I hope we get it together sooner rather than later because we can see the results of our actions in this new generation. They're so lost it's not funny anymore. They're confused about their sexuality. They're clueless about life, and they don't have any desire to work hard for anything. They want everything handed to them. I'm not going to say all, but most of this generation is like this. We, as Christians, must do better for those who are coming after us. We must be mindful of how we treat each other because this generation is looking for an excuse not to serve God with their whole heart. I have included myself because I am a Christian, a believer, and a follower of Jesus Christ. I have also done some things I'm not very proud of. This is the reason we are supposed to help each other and not judge one another so we can grow together as one and help build up someone else.

What I'm writing in this book will cause a few people to ask, "Why didn't you tell me?" or, "Why didn't you say anything?"

According to God, it wasn't time. I had to be okay with my story before I could tell it to someone else. I apologize, but I've had so many rocks thrown at me before, or shall I say judgment against me, for stuff I had no control over. I've always thought it would be the same with anyone else I told.

For the people who feel like rocks are now being thrown at them, they are. This is not about you; this is about me. I have been released to tell my story, not yours. And because no one listened to me as a child, it's now coming out. That's why there is no such thing as a secret. Anything that happens in the dark eventually comes to the light.

> *For nothing is hidden that will not become evident, nor anything secret that will not be known and come to light.*
> *Luke 8:17*

Just for the record, I loved my mom. But I had to watch her life spiral downward, and she was never able to be her true self. When she passed away in 2006, she was still wounded. She never sought her purpose, and she never recovered from all the abuse she endured.

WHO TOLD YOU THAT YOU WERE GAY?

I asked this question—not to condemn or judge but as a reminder of what the Bible says. The majority of this generation says, "I'm gay," but has no idea what it means. When I was a kid, my dictionary said gay meant happy. So, the dictionary was changed to fit a lifestyle to make everyone that says, "I'm gay," feel more comfortable and okay to say it, so we put a definition to it. I agree with what the bible says

> *John 8:7: When they kept on questioning him, he straightened up and said to them, "Let any one of you who is without sin be the first to throw a stone at her."*

> *Hebrews 13:4: Marriage should be honored by all, and the marriage bed kept pure, for God will judge the adulterer and all the sexually immoral.*

> *Romans 1:26-28: Because of this, God gave them over to shameful lusts. Even their women exchanged natural sexual relations for unnatural ones. In the same way the men also abandoned natural relations with women and were inflamed with lust for one another. Men committed shameful acts with*

other men, and received in themselves the due penalty for their error. Furthermore, just as they did not think it worthwhile to retain the knowledge of God, so God gave them over to a depraved mind, so that they do what ought not to be done.

Jude 1:7: In a similar way, Sodom and Gomorrah and the surrounding towns gave themselves up to sexual immorality and perversion. They serve as an example of those who suffer the punishment of eternal fire.

I remember when my daughter Tane' told me that she liked girls and boys. Then she later did what the enemy wanted her to do, and that was to say it aloud. She posted to social media saying, "I wish everyone would stop asking me, Yes, I'm Gay!"

My daughter had previously told me, and I told her what I thought about it. She was okay with that. However, she was upset when I told her to take the post down. She was more upset when I told her not to bring her girlfriend around me because I don't agree with her lifestyle. "I love you, as my daughter, but I don't agree. If you bring her around me, I will lay hands on the both of you." Of course, she felt some type of way about that. I gave her an example.

"If you were strung out on drugs, it would be the same thing. I love you, as my daughter, but I don't agree with your lifestyle. I would be trying to help you the same way as now."

My first question to her was, "Who told you that you were gay?"

She said, "Nobody told me that. I just know it."

I said, "Someone had to tell you that. As your mother, I didn't tell you that you're gay."

"What do you mean?" She asked!

"As a kid, you don't know your name unless I tell you what your name is. You don't know you're a girl unless I first tell you that you are. So how are you going to listen to another's voice? An unfamiliar voice at that, which is the voice in your head or the voice of the enemy. God said, 'My sheep know my voice and another they will not follow.' (John 10:4-5) Paraphrased

"You don't even know who you are. How can you put a label on your life? I'm forty-one years old and just finding out who I am. It would be different if I knew for a fact you already know who you are and what your purpose in life is." I then asked her, "Why aren't you fighting for your sexuality? You know you can tell that voice no."

She said, "I have been fighting for my sexuality; I'm tired of fighting."

"Wow, so you're just going to give up and be okay with that?"

"Mom, this is not my first time."

"I know that. Remember, I'm your mom."

Everyone's situation is different; but for me and my house, we will serve the Lord. We will try our best to follow the instructions the Lord has for us. I know my daughter, and she is not gay. She has revealed some things to me that she would have to say on her own. These are things that could possibly affect her opinion of who she is. Even things that happened when I was pregnant with her, like rejection. That I will discuss later in another chapter.

I believe there shouldn't be labels if there is a possibility of other things going on that can alter a decision. For example: If a guy has been molested by a man, he should be careful about saying he's gay until he knows for sure that he has dealt with the emotional and traumatic part of the situation. Also, he should make sure the incident no longer influences his identity or decisions. Meaning, there may be counseling needed and forgiveness. The same goes for girls.

In my opinion, this generation is so lost. They are picking up any identity they can find as long as it's fitting to them and who they think they are. For some reason, they just take it, wear it, and put it on themselves. Whatever the new thing is that's trending right now, they take it and put it on themselves as well. They want so badly to be themselves but don't know how or who to turn to. Social media is a good asset, but it has a big influence on the kids today and not always in a good way. I know because I've done it myself. I was my generation's lost child trapped in an adult body. I wanted so badly for someone, anyone, to tell me who I am. Pull me out of myself. I was so afraid to come out of myself, because of the things I had to endure. For years, it was my hiding place.

As a kid, before I could have a voice, it was taken away. Before anyone was able to validate me, it was taken away. Before they could tell me who I was, it was taken away. Before they could tell me that I was a child of God, it was taken away. Before they could tell me that I was going to be somebody one day, it was taken away. Before they could tell me that I was beautiful, it was taken away. I had no self-esteem, and it didn't take a genius to see something was wrong with me.

When I was about eight years old we lived in these apartments called The Algonquin Apartments. My uncle PJ was over visiting one day. I have no idea where my mom was or anyone else for that matter, but I was in the kitchen. He came into the kitchen with me and picked me up like he was happy to see me. But instead of it being a happy occasion, it turned into something else. Uncle PJ picked me up with his hands placed underneath my armpits. When he went to put me down, he held me so close to him that I was able to feel his manhood. I felt so dirty, and I didn't know what to say or do. I walked out and went to my room. This is the stuff that was going on in my family and the house I lived in. People talk about the drug addicts and alcoholics because those are things that can be seen with the natural eye. But with perversion and lust, a person would need a spiritual eye to see that type of sin or pay very close attention to those around you.

I had no sense of self because before I could even develop any esteem, it was taken away by molestation and perversion. It didn't happen once, but as a kid, that's what I was subjected to. Once it happened, I couldn't keep them off me. Men and women, family and friends, neighbors and strangers. The result of this was devastating. If someone told me I was beautiful, I couldn't hear them or believe them, because of the mess going on in my head. My focus in school was off; I cried all the time. I was angry, and I had unnecessary fights. I became very rebellious, selfish, and an excellent thief. I just wanted everyone to leave me alone, especially the people who abused me. I say I didn't have a voice because everyone would talk over me. They were too scared that I would tell on them once I opened my mouth. It was almost like when I saw everyone, I could see it in their eyes, "I wonder if she knows or does she remember?" It was almost like they were thinking, "Will today be the day that she says something?"

I never did because I didn't have anyone to tell. Everyone who was close to me was the ones abusing me. Of course, that meant I would be telling them on themselves and telling them on the others in the house.

So, I didn't tell anyone. If and when I did try and tell anyone, they wouldn't listen to me or believe me. So, I kept quiet. I believed I was not important enough for someone to hear me. I knew I had to find an escape, which was books. I read every book the elementary school library had that I could get my hands on. My favorite book was *Are You There, God? It's Me, Margaret* by Judy Blume. It gave me something to believe in and I felt like maybe there was hope for me. I loved going to school because that was my escape too. We used to pray at school, and that would make me feel okay for a little while. In my opinion, lawmakers shouldn't have taken prayer out of school because they never know what is going on at home. School was safe for most of us and provided a good hot meal.

Having no identity or self-esteem was not healthy for me or healthy for the people around me. After a while, people began to notice I have nothing to offer them but hurt. Because that's all I knew and had known. I probably wouldn't have labeled myself considering I wasn't sure of my identity.

One day in elementary school, I had an encounter with God. Back then, I didn't really know or understand about spirituality but because I was reading the book *Are You There, God? It's Me, Margaret,* I decided to implement it in my life to see if God was real. When I was alone, which was most of my childhood, I would say, "Are you there, God? It's me, Dorothy."

It so happened that after a long weekend, I went to school very hungry, I think I went late as usual because I didn't have breakfast. By the time lunch came around, I was starving. I was standing in the lunch line waiting to eat, which felt like forever. At that time, there were no air conditioners just big utility fans. It was so hot from the cooking, and the heat from outside made it worse. The heat affected me so much I fainted. Hungry and hot for me was a bad combination. No one noticed I was lying on the cafeteria floor. But I did notice, as I was looking up, there was a bright light and clear skies. It was peaceful. I felt nothing but love; a love that I had never felt before. Then there was a shift, and I was looking down at myself. I couldn't help but think, "Am I dead? Did I die?"

I was extremely excited. I wanted to scream, "Yes! I no longer have to deal with all the abuse anymore!" All I wanted was to die and be done with life and the people around me. I wanted to stay there and never leave.

I figured if I were no longer here, no one would notice me being gone. They didn't notice me anyway, so they wouldn't miss me. It was like time stood still because as I woke up in the cafeteria and stood back in line, it was like nothing ever happened. I went through the line like normal. Something did change within me that day, though. After that day, I knew I could handle anything that came my way because God was with me. I was like, He is real! He is real!

When I was home, and we had lots of company over, as usual, I knew I would be touched by someone. It was a usual thing when company was over. So, when I thought I heard someone coming, I would get scared, and I heard a voice say to hide in the closet. I obeyed the voice and went hiding in the closet as instructed. We didn't have dressers for our clothes, so my closet floor was full of them. My closet was my new hiding place. I would go and hide under all those clothes to keep the drunks off of me. I lived in constant fear, but I went on like nothing was wrong.

I couldn't stop; I had to live for some reason. I only wanted to die sometimes but not as much as before the encounter with God. The desires were slowly going away. I would try smothering myself in the pillow. It wouldn't work, so I couldn't do that.

Then the abuse changed to happening while going with my mom on her little outings with her friends. That's a whole other story within itself. I will discuss it later in another chapter because that was another issue which shaped my life. When I see people who are not being themselves and are doing things to hurt themselves, I wonder, what is their story? Because there is a reason for their actions.

That is why I wouldn't judge anyone because I may need to find out what their story is first. I would ask questions like, "Why do you act the way you do?" So, when I say to my daughter that I understand, I really do. I get it; that could have easily been me.

I only have a few people that I can actually call cousin. So, when my cousins came around, I would get excited and couldn't wait to hang out. Well, my cousin Mona came down from Chicago to visit her mom. She wanted me to spend the night at their house. I asked, and I went. We didn't spend a night at anyone's house all because people have too much going on in their homes. Heck, I had enough going on in my house, so I knew firsthand.

My cousin was much older than I. I was so happy to have her here because everyone in our family lived in the country. I went over there, and the same thing happened there, too, I woke up to her mouth on my female parts. I couldn't help but think, *Is this all I'm good for? Is this all I'm put on this earth for?*

I was trying to fight her off me. She was begging, "Please, let me finish." I had to leave the room to sleep on the couch in the living room. I never went back over there again. And I never told anyone about that incident either.

Once I got to middle school, and we moved out of The Algonquin Apartments, where most of the abuse took place, I forgot about the closet. I was lost and confused without anywhere to hide. We then moved to the Forest Place Apartments. I begin to hide in my mind; everything became internal for me. I no longer expressed myself outwardly. I can say now that was when my toughest battle began. I started to hear another voice that would say to me, "You like girls."

I would wonder where the voice came from because it didn't sound like God at all. It was a constant battle of mine. I then heard, "Tell it, NO! Tell that voice, NO!"

I heard God say, "That is confusion."

This is what was going on in my mind; it was like having good on one shoulder and evil on another shoulder. I had to decipher one voice from the other. Every time I heard that voice say, "You like girls," I would say, "No, I don't! That's a lie."

After a while, I finally defeated that struggle with the help of God. Then came the other stuff. I began to notice all my friends liked the same sex. The girls liked other girls, and the boys liked other boys. But not me, I had a different appetite. These were my friends, though, and I couldn't understand what was happening around me. I began to hear rumors about them and people saying they were gay. I would have to take up for my friends. Big Joe, the man my mom said was my dad would tell me that one of my friends who was a boy named Quinn, "Your friend is gay."

I said, "No, he isn't. He has a baby." Little did I know; it came out later that he liked guys.

Uncle PJ lied on me one time. He said to Big Mama with a smirk on his face, "the girls are after her," and I was like, "What are you talking about?" There were no girls that liked me. He was just finding little stuff to say to me to keep me distracted.

That was another reason why I stayed away; there were always rocks being thrown at me in the form of false accusations, which I now know were distractions. I began to see things and didn't have anyone to talk to about them and didn't understand them either. When I was asleep at night, I would have dreams. Everything around me was dark, but I was still able to see.

One day, I was over at my Big Mama's house and sitting at the table. It was just a normal visit, or so I thought. I told her I was able to see in the dark and didn't understand what it meant. Her comeback was, "Are you gay?"

I said, "No! Why would you ask me that?"

She replied, "I was just asking."

Still, she never helped me with my question and never gave me a valid reason for asking me was I gay. That was another distraction from the enemy. I begin to equate me being able to see things in the dark in my dreams with being gay. I left it alone and didn't want to have anything to do with it. I never asked again. And neither did she.

What no one knows is that the enemy was trying to get me to stop fighting for my sexuality and give in to what the voice was saying. But I was not going to do that. He used my family, who was open to being used by the enemy, to cause me to stumble and fall. Uncle PJ would try to say little stuff to try and make me think I was into girls, too. But that was a lie, too, and I knew it. As time went by, I understood the distractions were to deter me from speaking my truth about them. If I were distracted by the rocks they were throwing, I wouldn't focus on the memory of them touching me. They made sure I had no chance to bring up the incidents at any time.

Later, after I accepted Christ, I learned things during my time of devotion. God reminded me that when I was younger, it was Him, and not the enemy, who surrounded me with those friends that liked the same sex for my own protection. It was all a ploy to throw off the enemy. I had to hide in plain sight. If I looked like who I was fighting against, the enemy would think he had me. The plan was to get information on how to defeat the enemy from the enemy. Because to the enemy, it looked like he had me where he wanted me. But that was a lie. God had me all the time, I didn't know back then, but I do now. God then took me to Daniel in the Lion's Den. I wept like a baby, only because it was refreshing to know that at the hardest time in my life, He was still thinking of me. *Daniel 6:16-23*

After I defeated the issue concerning my sexuality with the help of God, He brought new friends into my life. I would still encounter some girls with that same spirit, and I saw them looking at me like they were familiar with me. I could hear myself in the spirit, telling their spirit, "No, I do not like girls and stay away from me."

They would never approach me. But they looked confused; they knew what they saw was the same thing on me that was going on inside of them. I know it may sound weird to most people, but to me, it wasn't. This is how God trained me. It's called a familiar spirit. When I have a spirit on me, it will attract someone with a like spirit.

This is how I learned how to battle in my mind. I told myself:
I'm a weapon of mass destruction because I'm one of those

people who confuse the enemy instead of the enemy confusing me. This is me fighting for my identity in Christ.

> *2 Corinthians 10:4 For the weapons of our warfare are not of the flesh but have divine power to destroy strongholds.*

> *Ephesians 6:12 For we do not wrestle against flesh and blood, but against the rulers, against the authorities, against the cosmic powers over this present darkness, against the spiritual forces of evil in the heavenly places.*

I then began to think there was something wrong with me, *why does everyone want to abuse me?* I was almost raped by DJ, one of the guys in the Forest Place Apartments where we lived at the time; I thought he was my friend. I was walking down the sidewalk one day, and he called my name. I answered. It was so easy for him to get me in his apartment because my friend Addy was dating his first cousin Benny. Benny didn't live in the apartments, but he would visit as often as he could. When DJ called my name, I didn't think anything of it. He said Addy wants you, she said come here. I had to fight my way out of his place. He tricked me into thinking my friend was in his apartment, and she wanted me.

Once I was in there, I knew it was a trick. The difference between being molested and being raped was the molesters groomed me into being okay with allowing them to touch me because they had somehow proved they loved me. They patiently worked up to what they wanted to do with me and had been watching and befriending me.

Now the rapists were whole other beasts themselves. The rapists were automatically aggressive and made a fight come out of me because of how they attacked me. My mind told me they were trying to take something from me. With the molester, I didn't realize the abuse until it had already happened because it was so calculated and strategic. I thought it was love until I felt the shame of it. I believe it kept happening to me because I never told anyone about the repetitive abuse. So, the spirit within them was the driving force that spoke to them and said it was okay for them to do it because I wouldn't say anything.

I found out a couple of years later that DJ went to jail later for raping his own girlfriend. So again, I believe God was watching over me and helping to fight my battles.

Another time, I was with some of my friends Maddie and Pearl, and we were on our way to The Mezzo Apartments to see this guy I was dating name Enoch. We were at a car wash off of Mezzo Street, and my friends were talking to these guys name Abel and Trent, and the other guy named Monty automatically thought I wanted to hang out with him. This fool tried to kidnap me. We were fighting him off; I got my hand and fingers smashed in his car door because he tried to push me in his car. His friends had to tell him to leave me alone. "She doesn't want to go with you man." He acted like he didn't understand the word, NO! My friends helped me get away from him and we left in a hurry. I had never met him before that day. I later heard on the news that Monty committed suicide because he was going to jail for the assault and rape of another girl. God was looking out for me again.

To me, these were all situations that were trying to distract me from what I was really supposed to be doing. When I say I understand that everyone's situation is different, it is. I'm giving my examples to show how the enemy distracted me from my purpose. I can only speak of my firsthand encounters and some that I've seen. I can't judge anyone for their struggle because I was able to say no to what tried to confuse me. I don't know what would have happened if my first sexual encounter had been with a woman. But it didn't happen like that; it was with a man. So that is what I looked for and fought for, with the help of God, against anything else that tried to tell me otherwise. I never told myself I was gay, and I never agreed to it. But I did fight for my sexuality because deep down inside, I knew homosexuality was wrong.

I came across Darren this guy at a company I used to work for called ISBO. He was cute. We talked every now and then. One day, we were at the office casually talking, and Darren said that he was going out of town to marry his boyfriend. I said, "Dude, you know that morally, you're wrong."

He looked at me with a small grin and said, "I know," and walked off.

So deep down inside we all know right from wrong, but we choose to do what we want to do or do what makes us feel good. He came back a couple of days later and was married. I was wowed! I still talked to him and didn't judge him, but I wondered about the spiritual fight he had to go up against with making that decision.

There was an older lady name Nina who worked at ISBO with us. I gave her a ride home one day and I found out she knew Darren very well. They work in the same department and they talked all the time. She told me that Darren's mom used to scream and holler at him. She talked down to him and talked bad about his dad to him. I just said, "Wow! So that's where that came from." That is what it looks like to emasculate a man, and if his dad wasn't around than he may have felt rejected. This too can cause someone to waiver in their identity. Then comes the fear, lust, pride and maybe even insecurity.

Before we label ourselves, make sure we know exactly who we are first. It's dangerous to say I'm this and that before we know for sure. One thing I know for sure is I'm a child of the most-high God, and He works in my favor. I know for sure I'm an entrepreneur. I know for sure I'm a mother. I know for sure I'm an author of many books to come. I know for sure I'm a good friend to have. I know for sure I'm a wife and not a side chick or just a girlfriend, and I know for sure I am a warrior. I know for sure I'm not gay. I know I'm not condemned. I know I'm not confused, and I know I'm not a prostitute or any of the other names I've been called throughout my life here on this earth.

All I'm saying is, I would find out who I am first before I say, "I'm gay!"

I pray that as you read this, the holy spirit will speak to you, and that a spirit of holiness will come upon you in the mighty name of Jesus.

I renounce all lust, perversion, immorality, uncleanness, impurity, and sexual sin in the name of Jesus!
I renounce all hatred, anger, resentment, revenge, retaliation, unforgiveness, and bitterness in the name of Jesus!

I renounce all pride, haughtiness, arrogance, vanity, ego, disobedience, and rebellion in the name of Jesus!

I receive the spirit of holiness in my life to walk in sexual purity in the name of Jesus! (Romans 1:4 paraphrased)

I break all spoken curses and negative words spoken over my life by others, including those in the authority in the name of Jesus!

WHO TOLD YOU THAT YOU WERE A PROSTITUTE?

My truth is that my mom Shae was a prostitute. It took me years to be okay with saying that. I guessed if I said it, it would tell where I came from. I thought to admit it would come with judgment.

It's a lot of stuff I don't care to remember, but somehow it comes back to my memory when God feels like I can handle it. I do remember that when certain people in my family would try to tell me stuff, they were distracted from telling me, or I made sure they knew I didn't want to hear it. I know some stuff my family made sure to tell me to keep me in the pit I was already in. They were there to remind me how much of a mess my life was; like I had something to do with shaping my own life. If I had a choice to pick what I wanted my childhood to look like, I wouldn't pick these situations for me or anyone else for that matter. I pray that no one has to ever go through what I went through. It was so ugly and heavy to carry, I don't wish that on my worst enemy.

My mom being a prostitute has shaped my life because I was her daughter, and I lived with her. That thing got passed down to me like it was an inheritance. I didn't realize then that it was called prostitution. As a kid, I didn't really put a label on people like that. I saw a lot but didn't say too much about it. The Algonquin Apartments where we lived was crazy chaotic. There were people at our house all the time; we had no peaceful sleep. There were always parties, drugs, drinking, fighting, and laughing; just loudness throughout the night. My mom was gone all the time, and everywhere we went, the men loved her. My mom was beautiful. She was what the men today would call a "dime piece." She was fair-skinned with long legs, and a beautiful smile that could light up any room. She only had a few female friends; maybe two or three she really messed with. I didn't like my mom's lifestyle, but how else was she supposed to pay the bills and feed us? No one else was helping take care of us. We had Big Joe, but we couldn't really tell. At least not according to the way we were living. He barely came around only when it benefited him.

Certain incidents helped shape the person I am today and how I think. One day, my mom Shae, came to Hilton Elementary, the school where I was going at the time. She felt like she had to see me and interrupt my class time. I believe I was in kindergarten because it was nap time. There was a knock at the door and the teacher called me out. I went to the hallway, and she was at the door to see me. She had on shorts that showed the darkest part of her booty, a halter top that crisscrossed in the back, and high-heeled shoes. Clearly, she was on the pills again. Mom was so high; I don't believe she realized where she was. The principal was rushing down the hall and telling my mom, ma'am, ma'am you can't walk around the school like that. He had to give her a shirt to put on and cover her nakedness. Now imagine what that does to a little kid. Well, I can say that I was beyond embarrassed; my little heart was just messed up.

Why couldn't I have a normal life? I didn't know what normal was because no one was talking to me or telling me it would be okay. Or letting me know that other people also had issues. I always thought it was just me living in a nightmare. My younger brother Tay lived with us, but he was a baby. My sister Kam and my older brother Ray left to go live with Big Joe. I was pretty much alone.

Some people might ask why I didn't go with them to live with Big Joe. Well, this is how it went, I was there for a little while, but my Big Mama's house was overcrowded. The reality was Big Mama and her sons, didn't really want us there, or just me, I didn't really feel welcomed. They may have been upset because Big Joe was never there with us. I decided to go back and live with my mom. I can tell when I'm not welcomed in someone else's home. And I got tired of everyone talking about my mom like she was trash from the street and no one was trying to help her. The problem was that they couldn't control her. I found that out later because that's how they tried to also do me. I consider myself a wildflower who can't be confined to one spot or area because I will outgrow everywhere I'm put. I can't be put in a box because I'm busting out of it as well. When you think I'm just limited to that one thing or one area, I'm not. I'm coming out.

Big Joe didn't really want me to live at Big Mama's, either. He wanted me with my mom for his own selfish reasons. He wanted me to watch my mom and then ask me what she was doing and if she had a boyfriend. He did this numerous time, but I remembered this particular time because it was the first time I had made good grades. I was in the 4th grade and Big Joe picked me up from the apartments and took me to Andersons, the neighborhood store. I was so excited he came to see me, because I wanted to show him that I had made good grades at school. Once we stopped at the store, I showed him my grades. He looked at them nonchalantly and then asked me about my mom. With my sad face, I told him she was still taking pills and gave them to him. I'd found them in her coat in the closet. The disappointment I felt was heart wrenching.

The part that hurt most was realizing he wasn't there for me but wanted to know about my mom. After that, I never cared about my grades again. They didn't care, so I didn't care. I didn't make any effort to get good grades; I just got by to pass to the next grade.

What he wasn't telling his family, the ones he was sitting up talking about my mom with, is that he really did love her. He just couldn't make a prostitute his wife. It was bad enough he had kids with her. I'm sure Big Mama went in on him about that.

Let me tell a little about my mom's background. My mom is originally from Maaco, Texas, where she lived with her Aunt Mae and Uncle Nev. Her dad was J.R. Smith, and her mom was Lore Franks, I think. I believe her mom died while giving birth to her. Anyway, I have no idea what happened to her dad. But her mom was in the Navy or one of the military services. Maaco is a little country town that didn't have a lot going on. Everyone knew each other, and some of Big Joe's family lived there also. The story Big Joe told us was that he won my mom in a bet. Now why kids would need to know that, I don't know. I've heard she didn't have a big family to protect her. She was mostly around Big Joes' family, which consisted of mostly men. They treated her badly; they used her up and then talked about her when she wasn't able to recover from their abuse.

Let me say this before I go on—the reason I use words like 'I'm told' or "I heard" is because the only way I was able to get to know my mom was by her getting drunk or high. Then she would start babbling. She didn't sit down and talk to us about her past or her family. Big Joes' family made sure we only knew about the bad parts of my mom and where she came from. In my opinion, it was to keep the blame away from Big Joe. My mom Shae did not walk us through things and teach us; we had to pick stuff up along the way or by watching. At least that is how I learned.

My mom came to San Juan thinking she was going to have help from the man who got her pregnant. Everyone blamed my mom for everything, but no one made Big Joe take responsibility for his actions. Our life was so chaotic that my oldest brother Ray couldn't walk for a while, and I heard someone say it was because my mom was taking pills while she was pregnant with him. He lived with my Aunt Polly for a while, and she helped him walk again. Aunt Polly said all she did was oil him down and prayed for him. All it took was prayer, love, and some attention. I thought it was weird that my Aunt Polly never came outside. She had no kids and no husband.

As a kid, I didn't understand what was wrong with these people around me. I found out later in my adulthood that a deacon in their church raped her. After that, she was never the same. That really messed her up badly. See how abuse can put a halt to a whole life? The fear that it causes is ridiculous.

That was just a little snippet of where my mom came from and the dysfunction I was in. Living with my mom was hard. But no one else wanted to deal with us or shall I say, deal with our dysfunction. My mom would leave all the time; I got tired of her leaving the house without me because when she would leave, I would get touched by the drunks in the house. We had all kinds of people living with us. We had the party house. And after a while, I thought it would save me if I went with my mom even though I didn't know where she was going. I would cry for her to take me with her, begging her not to leave me there with those people. It seemed that everyone would wait until dark to come in my room and take their frustrations out on me. Even the men who wanted my mom would be left at the house. If they couldn't have her, they would come and get me.

I found out it was even worse out in the streets with my mom. I went on jobs with her. She would go in the room with a guy, and sometimes I would sit in a chair, kicking my feet and swinging them back and forth while waiting for her to finish. Then we would go to another job.

She would get me little snacks here and there in between jobs. I would wait for her until she was ready to go home. I don't remember when it started. But I know I was no longer sitting in the chair waiting for her; she was now waiting for me. Usually, she would say, "Sit right here and wait for me. I will be right back."

This one job we went to, she left me in a room and told me to stay. A guy walked in, and I don't remember what he looked like. All I know is I didn't want to stay. All she said was, "Do whatever he asks you to do."

I didn't know what my mom did behind the door once it was closed, and I didn't want to know. I was just happy to be around my mom. But once she closed the door, who knew what that man was about to do to me?

As a kid, sometimes it's known when and when not to ask questions. This was my time to speak up and I did, I asked, "Why do I have to stay? Did I do something wrong? Why can't I just sit in the chair again?"

She said, "Stay."

I don't remember how she influenced me to stay. But I cried so hard, saying, "Don't leave me here. Please, don't leave me here with him. Don't make me stay here."

I don't know if it was the drugs that clouded her judgment, or she just needed the money. But she left me there and let that man have me. I don't remember how many times it happened; I just know it was enough to turn me away from her. I no longer considered her or those people my family. I felt alone and by myself. No one came to my rescue. No one helped me. I was bitter; I cried all the time. I was angry and didn't care about anyone outside of myself. I knew I had to protect myself. Why? Because there was no one else that was going to do it.

I always thought something was wrong with me. The shame I felt was unexplainable; the fear I felt was that someone was always going to come to my room and get me. What I didn't realize, as a child, was that I was holding someone else's secret. I didn't have anyone to tell, and it got heavier and heavier to carry. I didn't have an escape, so I began to act out. I was rebellious, stealing and fighting for no reason. I just did crazy stuff. No one else cared, so I didn't care. I just wanted to die. I just wanted someone to kill me and get it over with.

Once we moved to the new Forest Apartment complex and were around new people, I thought it would be better. It got worse. I found new friends. I got along with them, and we hung out. I was just glad no one was touching me anymore.

Then something new started happening to me. I started getting this visitation. I didn't know what it was at the time, but I do now. Because of the molestation, my body was introduced to a feeling I couldn't explain or control. Whenever I tried to sleep on my back, I felt like someone was touching me. I was waking up because I kept having these weird feelings.

At that time, I didn't know that it was called orgasm; I just thought I had a release. Once I realized what was happening, I would wake up, but no one was there. Some people may call it a wet dream. That is not what that is called. There is no such thing as a wet dream, and whoever made that up is a lie. That was a spirit molesting me.

Do some homework on the issue. If a visual is needed, look at the old movie called *The Entity*, it will give a visual of what I mean. This is only for believers because they're the only ones who may understand the movie and this situation. I felt so dirty and used every time it was done. This is the same way I felt after being molested by those grownups—ashamed, dirty, used, and abused. I would roll over and cry and couldn't tell anyone or explain to anyone. Why? Because I didn't know what it was, and I thought I was crazy. I just wanted it to stop. I tried to stay awake as much as I could and keep watch to make sure I was okay.

This went on for a while. It wasn't every night but every once in a while. I don't know if certain triggers caused it to come or not. It may have come from all the sexual secrets that came from the people in the apartment. I never paid attention to the times it would happen; I just wanted it to stop. I just know in the apartment we lived in, the atmosphere felt dirty. It was loud, stiff, and felt like something was always there. The grownups were drinking, babbling, and talking loud throughout the night. Sometimes they were fighting in the middle of the night. This kept us up at night also.

While living in the Forest Place Apartments, the day started out the same drinking and smoking, and we were all up late as usual. My Great Uncle Taft who was considered the alcoholic of the family did his usual drinking and babbling all night long. Uncle Taft was so drunk he urinated in the closet instead of the bathroom toilet. I thought that was so nasty and disrespectful. My mom was so upset but nothing changed. It was really hard to live there and get any sleep in that place. I noticed that everyone in Big Joes' family has lived with us at least once, accept him. He never lived with us; he would just come for a few days to lay up with my mom, and that was it. All the predators that were around knew this, so there wasn't any protection for us.

The only difference with living in the Forest Place Apartments was that my mom was no longer going on jobs. I didn't get the visitations after a while, but I didn't need them because then I started touching myself. I know that may be too much for some people to hear, but that is my truth. I found pornographic cartoons in my mom's room and started reading them. That became a habit of mine. I would live in her room and watch television. I barely went outside; but when I did, I stayed for hours. This was my escape because I had nothing else. I would get lost in the television and fantasize about the families on TV. I wondered why I couldn't have a normal life like those people. No one was telling me these shows were make-believe, so my fantasy and daydreaming went haywire. Even when I realized they were just shows put on by actors, I didn't want to escape the fantasy island. I was just trying to get relief from the reoccurring memories in my mind.

I finally started my cycle and didn't know what the heck it was, or what to do. I thought I'd done something wrong, so I hid it. I would use toilet paper to stop the blood. Then I remembered what we talked about in health class and realized this was normal. I felt a little better, but I still didn't have anyone to talk to about it. My mom found out because of my clothes in the back of my closet. She gave me books to read about my cycle, and that was it. I read them; and then, I stuck them in the closet with everything else.

I met a boy named Kojo, while living in the Forest Place Apartments and we begin dating and end up having sex. He was two years younger than me, but he looked older. We were just having fun with that puppy love. It lasted a few years. At the end of my 8th grade year, I begin participating in the summer work program for teens. The program required us to take classes half a day at the Antonian College and then go to our job locations the other half of the work day. I was located down the street from the college, at Callus Recreational Gym. While in the class one of the teachers Ms. Cathem asked me if I was pregnant. I said no, "What are you talking about?"

She said, "You look like you're pregnant."

I was like, *what is she talking about*? I just went on about my business and left that alone. When I got home I told my boyfriend Kojo about what the lady said, though.

He asked, "Well, are you?"

I replied, "I don't know. I still have my cycle, but it was lighter than usual."

He tried to push on my stomach to check for himself. I made him stop and told him to get his hands off me.

We were at the end of the summer, and it was time to go back to school. I was walking down the hall from one of my classes and my best friend Rat's sister Addy asked me if I was pregnant. Of course, I said no, I'm not pregnant, she said you look like you are. I just walked off and went to another class. I was wondering why everyone kept asking me that? I didn't realize having sex once could get me pregnant. Everyone kept asking me if I was pregnant because my body was changing. My pants were tighter than usual. My boobs and butt were filling out, and my hips were spreading. So, yes, I looked pregnant. I hid it for a while until I no longer had my cycle.

My best friend Rat, asked me seriously are you pregnant? I said I think I am, He then made me tell my mom Shae. I didn't have anyone else to talk to about it. Once my family found out about the pregnancy, I was told by Big Joe that I was going to have an abortion, and that was it. I was fourteen years old and didn't realize what was about to happen to my life. Big Joe came and took my mom and I to confirm the pregnancy. I was told by the doctor that I was already five and a half months. This meant I was too far along to get an abortion. Big Joe was upset and said I would have to stay in school.

At that time, I didn't know what the heck an abortion was. I barely knew what my cycle was. Again, they talked around me or at me and not to me. No one ever asked me if I was scared, or if I knew what was going on. They never asked my opinion about the pregnancy. They just took over and did what they felt like doing.

When Big Joe told Big Mama about the pregnancy, they came to the Forest Apartments where we lived. She had never been there before, but she came to see me. I got a whooping from Big Mama for being pregnant. I was called a prostitute, wh***, and b****. I was told I was just like my mom and I was never going to amount to anything. That's when it dawned on me that Big Mama really didn't like me. My mom got a beating and so did my older brother Ray because it was his friend.

It was Christmas day December 25, 1990, and we went to Big Mama's house to eat and I ate like a pregnant person. Once we got home I laid in my mom's bed watching television by myself. I begin to feel this pain in between my legs and didn't realize what it was. I began to cry and moan and tell myself you can take it, don't let them see you sweat, they will just talk about you. This was my mind set for my family never let them see you cry. It only lasted for a little while, after a few sharp pains I went to sleep. I had a doctor's appointment the next day and he sent me to the hospital saying that I had already dilated a few inches. I was like oh okay, that's what those pains were. I never asked what the dilation meant, I just followed my mom. Once we got there they signed me in and gave me a room, I had my baby that same day 12/26/90 about 10:00 that night.

I had the baby over Christmas break, so I didn't really miss any school, I was fifteen with a baby no job and no money and a baby daddy that was not old enough to work. What a life? I didn't know what to do with her, so I just tried to love on her the best I knew how, she was mine and no one could take her from me. I would let her sleep on my chest and I could feel her little heartbeat. It was beautiful.

I noticed I begin to get good at hiding stuff, and that was weird for me. I didn't notice it right away, but secrets became my identity. And the devil knew it; I was a secrets keeper.

After I had my baby, it was all downhill from there. I became very promiscuous. I wouldn't keep a boyfriend. I only messed with the guys I chose. If he liked me, I wouldn't mess with him unless I wanted to teach him a lesson. If he were pressing me to be his girlfriend, I would mess with his head by sexing him and leaving him alone. I would never mess with the same guy more than once. If you ever heard of the term "love them and leave them alone?" That was definitely who I was at that time in my life. I didn't know anything about a relationship. The relationships that were modeled around me were one-night stands.

Big Joe would only come around every once in a while, but only to lay up with my mom. That is what I saw, and the adults would judge me for how I acted without asking themselves about what they had modeled in front of me. I was still picky, though. I wouldn't mess with anyone I deemed to be too clingy. He had to be of a certain caliber which, for me, meant dark and handsome. No kissing and no holding hands.

The only thing that probably confused people was the fact that I didn't really care about a lot of attention. I was still very quiet. If I liked one guy, I would study him and make sure he noticed me.

I was a beast, and I didn't care. Now I did have a few crushes, but I didn't know how to talk to them. I didn't trust anyone enough to tell them about the crush. So, I never told anyone, which is pretty sad, because I didn't have anyone to confide in. As a matter of fact, there was no one on the earth that I trusted growing up. I had friends but still not enough to tell them my deepest, darkest issues. I didn't want to be judged. I kept it to myself a little while longer. As I got older, nothing changed; the promiscuity grew more and more. Same issue, new people, new places, and new faces.

The wilder I got, the more my family called me out of my name. This made it worse because I would rebel and say, "Oh! So, you called me this and that! Okay, I will act like it!"

I couldn't feel anything anyway; I was just hurting my body. The only thing is that I never took money because it would have made me feel more like a prostitute. I know people may say that I might as well have gotten paid for doing it, but that is not how I was thinking. I just wanted the pain to go away. I could take care of myself; I didn't need anyone's money. I was trying to feed the spirit that was controlling me. I needed someone—anyone to take the pain away. However, it never worked. I never got help, and no one ever came to my rescue.

As a young girl, I didn't see myself as marriage material. I learned early not to mess with a guy who had a girlfriend or anyone that my friends were messing with. There were a few times that I did get bored with the guys I messed with. They wanted to keep me, and I didn't want to be kept. I began messing with married men. It was fun for a while to sneak around with them until it happened to me. Remember, I was good at keeping secrets and the enemy new it. My whole mindset changed about messing with married men when I got married. Why? Because I didn't want anyone to do that to me. When the tables were turned, it wasn't such a good feeling.

I never approached a man about cheating on his wife; I thought it was more on him than me. He was the one in the relationship. But that was a lie, and something I was not very proud of. I now know to send that joker home if he tries to come for me. Once I became part of the wives' club, I thought the women who were cheating with my husband, should have sent him home. I believe all women should think like that. If we send the men back home to their wives, then who will they cheat with? But it's because we don't know our worth. We just take whoever we can get even if it's wrong or hurtful to us.

My mom Shae had kids with Big Joe and was never married to him. She became the woman on the side because he married other women and came back to her every chance he got. It was only because he knew she wouldn't tell him no. This is the thing that opened the door for me to believe it was okay to have a man come in and out of my house without ever marrying me. I learned it by watching how Big Joe treated my mom. The hard truth is Big Joe never saw my mom as marriage material and probably never will.

The healing comes when we, as women, are okay with the fact that every man is not going to like us. They're not going to see us as their wife. Somebody will, though. Some people are temporary and only in our lives as lessons for our growth. They shouldn't be looked at like a permanent situation. Be okay with letting go of what hurts you. We're prolonging our growth process.

For example: We're holding a flower with thorns in our hand, and we don't want to let go. It's special to us because, it represents the person we love, and we keep squeezing so tight that the thorns begin to pierce our hands. We can see with our eyes that our hand is bleeding. That means let it go because we're hurting ourselves.

If we can look on the inside at our hearts the same way, we could see our hands on the outside. We can see that the relationship we are in now is just hurting us. That means let it go. It's only going to hurt for a little while. This is a part of our process. Let it go. If we don't let it go, we will never meet anyone else and have a healthy relationship. Believe me, I know. Me Too. I had to go through the process as well.

I have been called every name in the book by my family alone. After a while, I just stopped acting like I cared what they thought about me. I began to ignore them and let their comments roll right off my back. I finally realized that I would never be good enough for them, and they will always see me as my mom instead of me. The only thing I didn't understand was how they could hate me for being like my mom. When they left me over there to be taught by her. This mistreatment went on for years; I would get cursed out for the simplest stuff. If my siblings and I got in trouble, it was all my fault. For example, we were all selling drugs out of the Forest Place Apartments. That was the second time we moved out there. We lived out there for years we were just at a different apartment number. Once Big Joe found out, I was the only one who got cursed out. Like I was the one who influenced the older siblings. I'm the youngest, so how could I influence them? I was like okay; I see how it goes. I was threatened numerous times about getting my daughter taken from me by Big Joe.

I couldn't help but think, *They can't take my daughter from me. I'm not unfit, so don't threaten me.* The big deal for me was never to allow any man to meet my daughter. I wouldn't bring anyone around her. I was scared for her to be around my own family. So, no one else was getting close either.

Even though my daughter had everything she needed, I was considered unfit by my own family. She had clothes, shoes, and many books to read because I was big on reading. I would read to her every night before she went to sleep. We would have pretend tea parties with cups that changed colors. But folks didn't see that; they just wanted to call out all the bad stuff I was doing to keep me in the pit that I was already in. All I ever wanted to hear was, "I'm sorry. Are you okay? Or ask, why do you act like that, and do you need help with something?" "Do you need someone to talk to?"

I never heard it and probably never will. Growth for me is never stopping and learning how to keep going even when I don't get the apology. I had forgotten about all the traumatic things that happened when I was younger. I pushed it to the back of my mind. I know now that it was because I didn't know how to heal on my own.

When I was about twenty-two years old and doing pretty good with my life, I just so happen to be over to Big Mama's house sitting at the kitchen table and minding my own business. She decided to blurt out your mom was a prostitute. I was like okay, so what does that mean. She couldn't answer me; she walked into her room as if nothing ever happened. I have to admit, I was hurt because she was digging up my mom's dirt. But she never told me why she was so bitter and mean. There was no need to tell me that unless she was about to help me with something or teach me something. But no, it didn't happen. It was another distraction to get me off track.

At about the age of twenty-five years, my fiancé Denny and I went to the Fish House on Calgon Road. When we walked in, we ordered the catfish and shrimp plate with fries. We went to stand and wait for our food. As we were waiting, this grown man and I locked eyes. We were looking into each other's eyes, and he had the same eyes my family had. I was so scared and wondering why this guy was looking at me like he knew me. I was afraid, and then I realized who he was. This nasty old man was our neighbor in The Algonquin Apartments, and the first man to touch me. I think he was more afraid than I was because he was looking at me like my family did. I would bet he was thinking, "Is she going to say something?" Or, "I wonder if she remembers?"

I told my fiancé Denny, and he was so mad he wanted to fight the man. I told him no, let's get our food and go and we left. I never saw him again. I realized I had a lot of inner issues and so I decided to finally accept Christ. And after going through months of marriage counseling, a year later I got married. That was hard for me, too. My family made sure they showed me that, that wasn't good enough, either. I got a call from Big Joe complaining about me not inviting him to the baptismal my daughter and I participated in. I had at least two meetings for my bridesmaids and only two of my friends showed up. That let me know that no one really wanted to participate in the wedding. I was upset about the no-shows, but I couldn't let that stop me. We came up with the idea to just use our two kids. They found ways to distract me from planning my wedding. Big Joe made sure I knew he was not happy about the wedding and told me that my husband Denny would use me. I tried my best to ignore him and everyone else and kept going. I noticed that they didn't want me to be happy.

It was the holidays. My daughter Tane' and I walked in to Big Mama's house, and everyone was there. Big Joe, Big Mama, Kam, and a few of my uncles. I knew they were talking about me because as soon as I walked in they decided to go in on me. Just saying crazy stuff to me. I had darts thrown at me about unnecessary, irrelevant stuff. I don't even remember what it was about. That's how unimportant it was. It may have been about going over there so late or not coming at all; it was something to that nature. Like my husband was stopping me from coming over there. Just another excuse for them to distract me. I wasn't going to stand by and allow them to put me down, or the guy who had to be a role model to my daughter. I walked out the door, and Big Mama came running after me, saying, "It's the Holidays, don't go! I just lost my brother. We all need to be a family."

I said I am not staying in there with him. He could talk to you crazy but not me.

She said, "Big Joe doesn't owe you anything."

I told her, "Good, 'cause I didn't ask him for anything." All I know was I left and didn't go back for a while. It was a few years, as a matter of fact. They didn't really know my oldest son D.L. because I didn't take him around very much. They barely got to see my youngest Amon. I couldn't do it anymore. It was unhealthy, and I had to make the decision not to subject my children or myself to such treatment.

When I got married to Denny I thought I knew what I was doing and what to expect. I didn't really understand what marriage was about. It was harder because no one around us was married. I was unable to model what a healthy marriage and relationship looked like. Even though it lasted twelve years I was done at six. I bombed at that marriage, but I did take some lessons from it. I couldn't help but think I couldn't do anything right. I found out that getting married didn't get rid of my inner issues. The things

I thought I got rid of by getting married and accepting Christ didn't go anywhere. It was a good hiding place for a while but didn't change how I felt about myself. I wasn't happy, and he wasn't happy. I still had no self-esteem, I compared myself to other women. I was asking myself: Should I have what they have at this age? Should I look like that? Am I behind? I just wanted out so bad, so I decided to cheat. Then it came back—that same spirit that made me promiscuous before. After all those years, it was just waiting for an opportunity and an open door.

I had been in church and couldn't understand why it was not dealt with. I was a part of a deliverance ministry. So why was I still promiscuous? It didn't dawn on me until the church found out I was getting a divorce, and I was leaving the church. Lady J told me not to leave my husband at the time because I would be sleeping around with different men. Over twelve years and Lady J you never addressed this issue in me? Was it hidden enough for you as a prophet not to see it? Did you see it and not address it for your own selfish reasons? But suddenly now that I'm getting a divorce, and I'm leaving the church, you want to tell me about my issue? Wow!! Thanks a lot. And if you've never seen it before, why not pray right now since you're calling it out? Don't get me wrong, I am still rooting for the church to get it together, but some people are not capable of pastoring. I will keep trying to walk upright before God, but some leadership needs to check themselves and their motives.

I think some people get a kick out of me being down because as long as I walk with a limp, then it justifies that they're ahead of me. Anything to make them feel good about them being in their mess. It's very sad to say, but it's true. If they look in the mirror, they're worse off than I am. Let's just say the church was right; that funky spirit did come back to haunt me. It's almost like it was waiting for me. I got right back into the routine as if it never stopped. I was mad because I didn't want to do this anymore. I just wanted someone to get this off of me.

I'm serious, this spirit was chasing me down. My spirit was like an incubator for it. It used anybody to try and get me, men and women. I had to literally run for my life. I started doing what I knew; I began fasting and praying, but nothing worked. I was like what in the world is going on, and why isn't anything working for me?

I found out that I had to go through this process because God wanted to do something in my brokenness. I needed Him to work on my behalf. I was now able to feel like I never had before. I experienced emotions I had not felt in years. This process was ordained by God. I told myself, "Once I'm free this time, I'm never going back."

I had to let someone with authority pray for me and get this funky stuff off of me and help me get set free. This was all a result of a familiar spirit that I grew up with. It had never left. It was dormant because I was married and covered. When I was uncovered, this same spirit came to attack me and threw me off. I realized it was all a distraction to get me off of my course. I said this because prior to my deliverance, I wasn't fasting like I used to. I wasn't praying anymore nor was I going to church regularly. I just gave up on God for a little while during that period of time in my life.

But I do declare that I am an intercessor, and I will not be moved no matter what is thrown at me. I don't care about being judged or not; I'm so free right now. Deuteronomy 23:17 states:

No Israelite man or woman is to become a shrine prostitute.

I renounce all sexual sin that I have been involved with in the past, including fornication, masturbation, pornography, perversion, fantasy, and adultery in the name of Jesus!

I renounce all ungodly soul ties and immoral relationships in the name of Jesus!

I release myself from every spirit of whoredom in the name of Jesus!

I bind and cast out all seducing spirits that would come my way in the name of Jesus!

I break all curses of adultery, perversion, fornication, lust, incest, rape, molestation, illegitimacy, harlotry, and polygamy in the name of Jesus.

I present my body to the Lord as a living sacrifice (Romans 12:1paraphrased)

WHO TOLD YOU THAT YOU WERE AN ORPHAN?
(The Spirit of Abandonment)

As an abused child, I felt abandoned by the people who were supposed to nurture and raise me. Why? Because first, my mom left me to be abused by the people in the house and again in the rooms with some random guys. Then my siblings moved out of the apartment. Big Joe left me at the apartment to be abused. So, yes, I felt abandoned because everyone was able to leave the situation but me. I had to stay and endure the pain of abuse. So, yes, that was a legitimate feeling at that time. As I grew older, I noticed that even the guys I dated or talked to started going to jail or disappearing out of my life. Again, I felt the abandonment.

I've had so many people come and go out of my life, but there were some who were beneficial to my life when they needed to be. I was probably about nine or ten years old when we first moved to our own spot at The Forest Place Apartments after living with my Uncle Taft for a while. I met this girl name Junie, who was very nice, and we became friends. The reason I remember her was because of her family. She lived in the same complex as us, as a matter of fact, she lived right behind us. I could see her apartment when I walked out of our front door.

I was so hurt. All I needed was some refuge from the storm I was in, and they were it. Like I said before, our apartment was so chaotic, it was too crazy for any children to be there. When I first went to her apartment, she had everything I had ever wanted as a kid. I couldn't help but think, *They're rich or something.*

She had every Barbie doll a kid could want, even the Barbie swimming pool and all the board games I could think of. Everything was in its place with no disorder. The walls of her apartment were so white that it looked like no one lived there. This black girl had fair skinned and beautiful long hair that was combed every day. Her clothes were clean, and I'd rarely seen her outside. If she was outside, her mom was out on the front porch watching. Her mom was light skinned also and walked with a cane but only for a little help. I believe her mom only used it when she was on her feet too long.

I would go over to her apartment, and it was like they already knew it was a hiding place for me. I would just sit over there for hours and play with her and all her toys. Oh, my God! It was so quiet and peaceful over there. I just wanted to stay and never leave. I think her mom was very specific about letting certain people around her, though. I had not seen too many kids in their apartment. They would feed me, and never once did they ask me anything about my family situation. They just let me hide out there as long as I wanted. She also had a brother named James, who didn't live there, but he was like grown-up older. He came to take Junie out to eat and asked if I wanted to go. I asked my mom, and she let me go with them. He took us downtown to a Mexican restaurant, where we could sit down and eat. That was a first for me.

He had this genuine character about him, and I could see it. It's kind of hard to explain, and it may seem like it's not a big deal. But coming from someone who'd never had that before, it was a big deal. When he showed me some love by taking me with them, I was ecstatic.

There was an incident on the bus with the tire about to go flat, and the bus was smoking. My friend Junie and I were sitting on the side that was smoking. Her brother James told us to come sit over by him. When we did, the seat rattled, shook, popped up in the air, and the tire went flat. He was so upset and screamed at the bus driver, "Shouldn't you check this stuff before you leave! I got my sister on this bus. You better be glad she's okay."

I was thinking, *Wow she has someone to take up for her, too.* That was something else I was missing. Later, we made it home safely on a different bus.

I believe her mom knew what kind of situation I was living in. Like I said before, it didn't take a genius to see I was troubled. There was nothing but men living in our apartment. They were coming and going as they pleased. The crazy thing is they were all family. I was the only girl living there besides my mom. And when I had the chance to get out of there and go to Junie's place, I was out. I didn't have to think twice.

They were not like us, though. As a matter of fact, I don't even know where they came from. But they weren't from around there. And I could see they looked like they came from money. It didn't matter to me; I was just happy to have a real friend. We played like we were two kids with no worry in the world. We didn't teach each other any bad habits. And I didn't have to fight for my life over there. We were just kids, and it was beautiful.

I can't even believe I'm writing about this because I have never talked about this to anyone. It was a sensitive issue for me. Even as I wrote this section, I had tears rolling down my face. When I remembered that time in my life, I thought it was about all the toys she had and how clean her house was. But it was never about that, and the reason I never talked about her was that I was crushed when she left. She was my first real best friend. I never stole anything from them like I did everyone else. And they were the first people to see me. I mean really see me, Dorothy, and didn't judge me or my situation. They just saw me as a kid. I was hurt, but I was still just a kid. These people saw my hurt and still genuinely loved me.

I'm telling this part because as soon as she moved away, I immediately felt the pain. I went home, and I got picked on by Kam about my friend leaving. She never asked if I was okay or how her leaving made me feel. I was hurt and I felt like my family had just abandoned me. I just wanted to hang on kicking and screaming, but I had to let go. I lost my best friend; she left me here. I don't really remember why they moved but I believe they found a more peaceful and less aggressive environment to live in. Why couldn't I go with them? They were there just for that moment in my life, and I didn't understand then because no one explained it to me. I never forgot her, though. I just pushed those feelings and the memories to the back of my mind. She was like a sister to me, you know like the one I never had.

In our neighborhood, there were no mentors or teachers who showed me any love. The way we grew up—we had to learn how to survive; we didn't have time to feel sorry for ourselves. We got knocked down and got back up. I don't recall anyone calling Child Protective Services when we were younger and saying that we were being abused. The city wasn't coming to take kids from abusive households. We just dealt with what was going on and kept moving. The Bible says:

> *James 1:27: Pure and undefiled religion before God and the Father is this: to visit orphans and widows in their trouble, and to keep oneself unspotted from the world.*

Are we doing our part to help our kids/orphans or those that are abandoned? I'm not saying that if someone had stepped in, my life would have been so perfect. But I am saying that just knowing I had someone believing in me, would have helped. I used to run track in elementary and middle school. I had ribbons and certificates that showed I was trying to do something to escape my home life. Because no one ever showed up, by the time I went to high school, I didn't want to do it anymore. I dropped the class and never went to practice. No one else cared, so I stopped caring.

I can imagine how the kids feel in foster care knowing they have family out in the world, but they're deemed unfit to care for their children. So, the kids can't go home to their parents.

Are we rehabilitating parents and getting them help to get back to their kids if they are willing to do the work? If there are parents who aren't trying to do the work to get back to their kids, then just love on the kids. If I ever come in contact with those kids that are missing guidance I will do just that, love on them in spite of. If we're the teacher, the pastor, or just a parent, and your kid is their friend, do we ask the kids are they okay? Do they need to talk? Do they need anything? What happened to the village that's supposed to help raise the kids? I remember seeing Shellie one of the ladies I knew from my running wild days. I introduced her to my son and told her which one he was. I gave her permission to tell on him. I said, "If you see my son doing anything that is disrespectful, please either say something or let me know."

She said, "No, I'm not telling on these kids. I don't have anything to do with that."

I was wowed.

I don't know what her reason was for saying that. Maybe she'd had a dilemma in that area before, and it placed a bad taste in her mouth. Not every adult is that open to hearing anything about their kids, but I am. I don't get everything right, so I need help with mine. I try to make sure the right leaders/people are around my kids. But you have to be saying the same thing we're saying. If you're not willing to teach them anything, then what is your purpose in their lives?

If we see kids going down the wrong path, are we just letting them fall by the wayside, or are we making some attempt to help them along the way? Even if they don't listen, at least try. We can't save them all but, believe it or not, some really want help. I refuse to let any of my kids, or any kid I come in contact with, fail.

My Aunt Polly used to try to help my mom. She would comb my hair, buy us Christmas presents, and feed us. She even bought me my first bike with the banana seat. It was really cool. I was still in elementary school, but I had already written off everyone in my family. I was not trying to hear any of them, and I didn't care who they were. When they tried to discipline me, I was like yeah, yeah, whatever. I already felt like they'd allowed the abuse to happen, and no one said anything. Anyone could see the route I was taking, all anyone had to do was pay attention. The family forgot about me, but I was okay. I didn't need any of them. I said that because my older brother Ray had my aunt Polly who nursed him back to health. My younger brother Tay had my mom Shae because she favored him more as her baby. And my sister Kam had Big Joe. I was determined to survive without any of them.

The only person who would tell me they loved me was the drunk; Uncle Taft. And at the time, I realized he was drunk, so I didn't believe him. No one liked the drunk uncle because he told everyone's business; he knew what was really going on. He would always try to tell me stuff, but I wouldn't allow him to because I just wasn't ready to remember all the trauma. I think they kept him drunk, so he wouldn't tell, or he got drunk because he saw a lot of stuff that took place and didn't have any other escape. Or the stuff he saw, he didn't know how to handle it.

Abandonment was not a good feeling. I began to take it personally when everyone left my life whether the relationship was healthy or not. I just wanted someone on my team. I just wanted to know someone was rooting for me. Can I get at least one cheerleader on my team? It happened year after year, people were leaving my life, either they would stop calling, or we would have a fallout. Or I would notice I did all the calling and checking up on people. No one would check on me and, as the years went by, I was okay after a while. At least, I thought I was. I just had to walk away from some people because I had a new relationship with Christ.

Over a period of time, I had new friends and family. We were okay until I started paying attention and noticed that the relationships again, were unhealthy. Even though I knew this when they left, I was feeling some type of way because again, I thought it could be worked on. This happened a few times within a two-year span. I was fed up. I was at a new church, and the pastor had to call it out to my attention that it was abandonment I was dealing with. I never heard that about myself or anyone around me before. Otherwise, it would have been a thought of mine. Or shall I say I didn't know you could be delivered from abandonment. My pastor had to tell me that some people in my life didn't have the capacity to deal with the issues I had going on. They weren't equipped for the season I was going into. I was okay with that explanation. It helped me with a few questions I also had about leadership.

Again, I wanted to know why the last church I was in did not help me deal with these issues. Over twelve years, and I felt like I didn't get anything broken off of me. I didn't put all the blame on them, but if they want their leadership to grow, they have to deal with the issues that have kept them bound.

A year went by, and it happened to me again. I had to let Ruby go, I thought she was my friend. She had to leave my life the way the others did. I was okay this time; I saw some signs of an unhealthy relationship but didn't have time to deal with it. I was too busy. I thought I was going to take certain people in my future but God had other plans. I had to be okay with that.

I'm now in a healthy place to be able to let people, who are not healthy for me, leave my life. If I'm not healthy for them, I'm also okay with that. It just took me a while because of the abandonment I felt as a kid. It spilled over into adulthood because it was never dealt with. That is why I had to learn how to deal with an issue right then and there, otherwise, it would come back for me to fix it later. I couldn't let anything fester and take root because then it would become a part of my then identity.

With the abandonment or an orphan mentality, it made me feel alone in a world full of people. I would be in a room full of people and still felt alone. Why? Because I was just surviving and not living or existing. I didn't feel loved. I didn't feel validated, and I put on this survivor mindset that kept me from living. When I was in survivor mode, I was moving all the time and trying to make sure I got everything done, make sure I could provide, and make sure I let everyone know I didn't need anyone, and then it turned into pride.

I could never figure out why I never had a mentor or an adult to help groom me and to help me with my identity or my growth. When I finally accepted Christ as my personal Lord and Savior, I thought I'd found my much-needed mentor at the church. Boy, was I wrong. I looked for the leadership to help me grow. I gave permission to the leadership saying, "if I do something wrong please correct me." But I got nothing. I said in front of other leaders at a meeting on numerous occasions. But still I got nothing. I'm not bashing the church. It's just to show believers that we have to know who's in our lives, and it has to be the right people to get us where we need to be in life and or in Christ.

When I was displeased with my growth, I left. I was just as messed up as I was when I went to the church. For a while, I was upset because, to me, it defeated the purpose of being there if there was no growth. I did my part. I read my Bible, fasted, prayed, served, and helped other people as much as I could. I even gave leadership permission to correct me when I was wrong. I know I didn't get everything right. I did what I thought I needed to do to get to the next level in Christ. Once I left there,

I realized I was never going to have anyone help me. So, I said, "Forget a mentor. If I haven't had one by now, I'm never going to have one. And I'm okay with that."

All I'm saying is don't forget to ask people are they okay and mean it because when we ask, we have to be willing to offer help or a listening ear. Even if it's a kid, we never know when someone needs help. Especially the strong people—they need help, too.

I renounce all hatred anger, resentment, revenge, retaliation, unforgiveness, and bitterness in the name of Jesus!!

I forgive any person who has ever hurt me, disappointed me, abandoned me, mistreated me, or rejected me in the name of Jesus!

I bind and rebuke all familiar spirits and spirit guides that would try to operate in my life from my ancestors in the name of Jesus!

WHO TOLD YOU THAT YOU WERE POOR?
(Poor Mentality)

I used to hear stories about people saying when they were younger that their moms would make a dollar out of fifteen cents. Now that I'm a parent, I understand what they meant. Being poor is a mentality. I didn't know that before, but I do now.

We're only as poor as our minds allow us to think. We grew up in the projects, and everyone made the same amount of money. Those who made more finally got out of the projects. So how do we get out of that mentality of being okay with what's around us? I believe that is why the crime rate is high; everyone wants to be okay in their finances that they're trying everything to get the pay and the money they deserve to have as an individual. Even if it's illegal.

For a long time, I thought material stuff was love because that's what I was shown. Big Joe would buy us stuff on the holidays, and that was love to me. Allowing men to lay on top of me was love to me. That was my perception of love.

As an adult, we have to be careful how we portray love to the kids around us because they will make up their own perceptions. Especially if no one is telling them otherwise. I took the wrong perception into my adulthood not really knowing that it was a crutch for me until I got married. It was even worse when I accepted Christ because God began to show me who I was. I didn't know how to express what I felt on the inside, only because that was not shown to me. Expression was a real struggle for me; it was something I had to allow God to work on.

I've heard story after story where people have stated, "I didn't know we didn't have any money because my mom didn't ever say we didn't have this or that. Their moms made it look like they were okay even though they didn't have a lot. It's called improvising as an adult with kids. We still provide even if we don't have as much as everyone else.

Being a young child and having to be evicted from almost every apartment complex we lived in for different reasons, made me have a poor mentality. I begin to get so used to living like that, I figured, okay this is all it's going to be and that's it. It's discouraging to feel like I was never going to make it any further than where I was. Even if I thought like that as a child, I couldn't stay there in my mind because my mind will shape my whole atmosphere. I had to move away from that way of thinking. When I decided, this is not going to be my life, and mean what I say and mean what I think, then things around me begin to change.

Sometimes we had to live in the dark with our lights out for non-payment. This didn't happen once, it happened a few times. There was not enough money for the growing teenagers in the home, and the adults who lived with us. Because we were on government assistance, the state only gave our household a set amount of money each month along with food stamps. It was based on the number of people in the household. If we ran out before the next month, that was up to us to figure out the next step for ourselves.

We didn't have medical insurance like some people, but we had Medicaid. When I said we, I mean my mom, my two brothers, and my uncle, who was living with us. I said we had Big Joe; but it just didn't seem like it, because of how we were living. I remember one time going over to Big Mama's house, I don't quite remember how old I was at the time. But I walked in and on the kitchen table and there was an open envelop and there were insurance cards. This may not seem like a big issue to some, but it was an issue for me. For a long time, I was embarrassed about being on Government Assistance. I hated going down there and asking for help. And to see that Kam and Big Joe had health insurance that really crushed me. Why didn't he have us on health insurance, we're you're kids too. So, I thought! I guess that's just the way it went. It must have been a secret because when Big Joe saw me at the table, and the cards were sitting out he hurried up and grabbed them and put it in his pocket. You know the crazy thing about it, is he even had an insurance card for his youngest son. Whom by the way didn't belong to my mom or his wife.

We found out about this kid in a crazy way. My brother was walking to Anderson's grocery store and this lady walked up to him out of nowhere and asked him, "Is your name Ray" and of course he's a kid so he said yes. Then she asked, "Is Big Joe your dad"? He answered yes to that also. She took it upon herself to show my brother this picture of her and this kid saying, "This is your little brother, his name is Davey". She let him have the picture and he took it to my mom. She was livid. She couldn't wait to talk to Big Joe about this one.

I thought it was pretty creepy. That means this lady was watching for us and stalking us, trying to find out who we were. She caught one of us and decided to approach my brother. Today she would be considered a stalker.

People wonder why my mom was half crazy this is some of the stuff she had to deal with. On top of all that, we didn't have much. Our clothes weren't the best, either. In elementary and middle school, I remember having holes in my underclothes, socks, and shoes. It was embarrassing. One day I had to go to the emergency room, I had an ingrown toenail that was infected. I had to take my clothes off and I had on a pair of panties that were too big with holes in them. In order to make me feel better, the nurse told me, "It's okay, we all have that pair that no longer fit us."

She saw me trying to pull them up and hide them. It may not seem bad to other people. But when we were in lack all the time, it made us feel some type of way. It seemed like we would never get out of the rut that we were in. It was like having no vision for our future. We had no idea where we were going.

The Bible says: *Where there is no vision, the people perish: but he that keepeth the law, happy is he. Proverbs 29:18*

I always knew I was different, but I didn't always know I was going to get out of the mess I was in. Growing up with other kids who had a little more than us was kind of embarrassing. They would talk about their moms working and where she worked. I can't recall my mom ever working when we were elementary age. She said she did some home health work from time to time. But I couldn't tell because we still didn't have anything. We were evicted from one of the apartment complexes we lived in. I still don't know the real reason why; I'm not sure if it was non-payment of the rent or another reason. We had so much stuff going on in our apartment; it was ridiculous. All I know is that when we came home, our stuff was sitting outside. Talk about embarrassing. It was so embarrassing for me to come home and see all our stuff sitting outside.

We didn't have anyone to help us move our stuff, so we had to try to get the things we really wanted. We lost a lot of pictures and everything else we owned. We ended up living with my uncle Taft across the tracks in The Forest Place Apartment Complex. It was only a one-bedroom apartment, so that was not enough room. It was my mom, my little brother Tay, and me.

We slept on a mattress in the living room on the floor. He lived with us before, so why wouldn't he let us live with him. He really was the only one that cared about me. The older I got he was the only one that would tell me how I was when I was younger. No one else had any stories about me or was too afraid to tell me because that meant remembering what they did to me.

One time, he said I used to keep my room so dark that he would have to go in and open the blinds and the curtains to let the light in. I remembered because that was around the time I was depressed. I was only in elementary school. But he was right, and I knew it but no one else paid any attention to that. The only time I cared to listen to him was when he was sober. I thought that was the best time to hear the truth.

Nothing changed once we moved in to his apartment, drinking, smoking, loud talking and staying up all night. I know a lot of people do that when they have a party. But I'm talking about every day of the week and all-night long. There was never any peace. He didn't have a lot of money, either. None of my mom's friends had any money. So, everyone around them was broke and living off the government check every month. I just couldn't understand why none of these people worked and wondered what was wrong with them that they couldn't work. I know my uncle was considered disabled because he used a cane. I don't know about the other adults. Were they lazy or just mentally poor?

What I mean by mentally poor is, did they have a desire to do more or be more? Did they have their own dreams, goals and aspirations? If not, their mentalities may have been poor. I'm not judging anyone, but some people may not realize they are mentally poor. If we desire things that we can't afford, then we may be mentally poor. Life and money are not about things. Do we understand what a legacy is? We work for the next generation and so on. Someone also should have been working to leave a legacy for us. How many of us have had a business passed down to us from the previous generation? Or how many of us have had an estate passed down to us? I can say not very many. How many of us desire to follow in our parent's footsteps as a doctor, lawyer, teacher or public figure. I'm not saying we have to do these things but just seeing someone in those positions help to give us some direction. I'm saying this because we're spending all our money on unnecessary stuff that is not going to last, and it will not bring us or our next generation any joy.

After watching my mom and her friends do the same thing day in and day out. I vowed as a young teenager; that I refuse to be on government assistance all my life. This is not how it's supposed to be for me or anyone. I didn't really know what I was going to do, but I knew I wasn't going to sit up in the house all day doing nothing. If I were going to be sitting up waiting for a check, it wouldn't be from public assistance.

I'm not completely counting it out because it helped me with my transition at one point in time in my life, but it was for a limited time. Those benefits are temporary; it's not supposed to be for a lifetime. Some people take advantage of the benefits. Again, that's the poor mentality, and it gets passed down to the kids. Those benefits are put in place to help people in transition just in case someone doesn't know that.

When I would come home from school, and my mom and her friends were there already drinking and smoking, it was sad and disappointing to me. I would always say this is not going to be my life. I refused to allow it to be my life or the life of my kids. I never really thought about my future until a teacher at the elementary school asked the question. What does everyone want to be when they grow-up. I originally wanted to be a teacher, but I forgot about it as I got older. My mind was so clouded with anger, rage, and bitterness that I didn't have time to think about it. I just knew what I didn't want to be.

Don't get me wrong; I'm not saying my mom never had any dreams. But life happened and routed her in a different direction. She was an amazing mom when she wasn't drinking and smoking. June, who was one of my mom's friends, said "Your mom could have been a nurse, because she did all my homework for me when I had to work." That is why she helped my mom every chance she could. She was the only one I knew of that was really doing anything with her life. I just wanted to see my mom happy after seeing her so sad all the time. But she couldn't shake that life of a poor mentality.

If all my friends are doing the same thing I'm doing, which is nothing at all. Then who's going to be the first person to get out. Or the person to show me it's more out there than what I'm doing. My mom never thought like that, and neither did her friends.

After I had my baby, I didn't have money. I stayed in school, so I didn't work. I received benefits through government assistance with my mom because I was underage. I did have some help from a few of my family members. I didn't realize it but, once I grew up and accepted Christ, He began to show me stuff. Where he was working on my behalf, he was the one encouraging those family members to help me. I thought they felt sorry for me. If it had not been for the Lord who was on my side.

When I was in high school, I received a check just to take a test. It was through the summer work program I participated in. It was called Youth to Adulthood. This would happen twice a year at the beginning and the end of the year. God made sure they picked me so that I would have money for my daughter. This check wasn't a lot, but it helped buy Christmas presents and birthday presents. Let's just say it came right on time. There were a few things that happened in my life that I couldn't explain. But I know now it was God, who was covering me. I believe that with all my heart.

As I got into my adult age my friends and I were doing the same things—just sleeping all day and hanging out all night. We all had kids and were just partying, selling drugs, and shopping. If I knew then what I know now, I would have used some of that money and put it away for a business. Because that, too, was a temporary situation. Many men try to make a lifestyle or career of selling drugs, but they can't.

First of all, it's illegal, and eventually, we get caught. We go in with a plan and get what we need, come up in the game, and get out. Flip our money another way, make our money make money for us. That's not how we did it though. We just spent and spent, until we couldn't spend anymore. Still the older dealers weren't teaching that either. They were doing the same thing. Some did put money away but what good is it you're not getting a return on it.

One day, I was hanging out at my friend Jewel's house with my brother Tay and another friend name Shon. I got tired of the drama, the mess, and sitting around doing nothing. I told my friends "I'm going to school. If you want to go, you better come on". I didn't wait for anyone, I just went. I remember seeing this school advertised on television. I got the information, and that Monday, I went to sign up and went to the nearby trade school called Career Enhancement. It wasn't some big college, but it helped get me where I was going. I couldn't lay around and keep doing the same thing with no results. When I have dreams and goals, I have to push myself. I don't know about everyone else but that's how I make it. There are levels to this thing called life. We have to know where we're at and where we're going so we don't get stuck.

I have been working since I was fourteen years old. I started working the summer with Youth to Adulthood program because I was tired of not having any money. Still, I didn't know what to do with my money. I would spend and spend until I didn't have any left. I didn't have anyone to tell me, "Stop playing with your money. Put it up so you can have money for later."

This went on into my adult life. I've always had jobs. But we had to move before we were evicted because I would be the only one working and didn't have enough to pay the rent. We've had our lights and water cut off. So, when I say it's a poor mentality that's what I mean. For a long time, I had to tell myself, "I am not living my mom's life. This is my life, and I demand more and better for myself."

I felt like I was doing the same thing my mom was doing when I was younger. Living how my mom was living, I wasn't on government assistance, but my mind was in that same way of thinking by living from check to check. I had to make a decision; not just for me but for my kids also. I wasn't happy with myself, and I knew this was not it for me.

There were some ideas I got from God, but I was doing more talking and writing them down than actually doing anything about it. I got tired of the same hustle and bustle of everyday life. I woke up one day, went downtown, got my Tax Id, a business name, and a bank account. I took my income tax (check) and started buying clothes in bulk. I would sell them at work, church, and the flea market or to anyone I came in contact with. I did that for about three and a half years. I got frustrated because I didn't have any help, and I was unorganized. I believe it was from the poor mentality because I should have pushed through the frustration. It didn't help that I had people around me who were jealous of my decision to want more for my life.

I found out I couldn't make people want what I wanted. They had to want something for themselves. I couldn't make them have my dreams and my goals. I know because that is what I tried to do for the people around me. But they didn't want what I wanted. My mind changed, but theirs didn't, it stayed the same. I had to move on and leave them behind. You can only drag people along for a little while, but then they drop off. I know now that it doesn't happen overnight. I'm trying again, and this time, I'm ready for real. I have more help, and I have a good support team.

I've had so much stuff broken off of my life from my past and having a poor mentality is one of them. I didn't want to be stagnated in old stuff that wasn't even mines to begin with. Most of the stuff I carried was from my family. I couldn't allow the old to take me down. I had to do something about it, especially if I wanted more. When my mind replayed the old stuff over and over again. I decided to do what the Bible says to do; I had to pull down every thought to the obedience of Christ. The Bible says it like this:

2 Corinthians 10:4-5: For the weapons of our warfare are not carnal but mighty through God for pulling down of strongholds, 5: casting down imaginations and every high thing that tries to exalteth itself against the knowledge of God, bringing into captivity every thought to the obedience of Christ.

The only way to get rid of the poor mentality is to change the way we think. Change the way we think about money and the way we think about people. Money and people are good resources. Everyone's situation is different, but we all need to change our mentality. I'm a good example because of the way I was raised and the environment I was brought up in. I was an emotional shopper. When I was mad or not feeling good about myself, I would shop and spend money. But I had to be healed from that, once I found out the root cause of it. That didn't stop me; it did hinder me for a while, though. I would always tell myself I was going to be Entrepreneur of the Year until I believed it for myself. That was just the beginning of my mind change. I begin teaching my kids about money, savings, retirement, and stocks. I refused to allow my kids to have that same poor mentality.

I break all curses of poverty, lack, debt, and failure in the name of Jesus!

Let every yoke of poverty be destroyed in the name of Jesus!

I command all hereditary spirits of poverty to come out of my life in the name of Jesus!

Jesus, You became poor, that through Your poverty I might be rich! (2 Corinthians 8:9)

I receive abundance and prosperity through the blood of Jesus!

WHO TOLD YOU TO COMMIT SUICIDE?

First of all, let me start by saying committing suicide is not the answer to any problem we may have. Please consider salvation first before considering taking your own life. Jesus saves, and He heals all wounds! I used to think it was selfish for someone to kill themselves. I forgot I was once there too. Because we feel like were taking away our pain but leaving other people in pain because we're no longer here. I now know that it's a spirit. For anyone who doesn't understand and have never seen the manifestation of it, then look at the movie called *Max Payne* with Mark Wahlberg. After taking the meds from the government. There was a spirit that started visiting the soldiers that made them want to commit suicide. There was a scene with the guy in the apartment and outside of his window was a demon that pulled on him to make it look like suicide. This is a demon spirit, and that's what the spirit of suicide looks like. No one else could see it but the soldiers. It's not visible to the natural eye. God is not okay with suicide; he put us here on the earth for a purpose.

It's wrong of us to try and take our lives before time, because it delays that purpose.

> *Ecclesiastes 7:17: Do not be overly wicked, nor be foolish; Why should you die before your time?*

> *Deuteronomy 30:19: I call heaven and earth as witnesses today against you, that I have set before you life and death, blessing and cursing; therefore choose life, that both you and your descendants may live;*

> *Psalm 147:3: He heals the brokenhearted and binds up their wounds.*

I used to want to die all the time, so I know how bad it can get, I just didn't know how to do it. I had never seen anyone be successful at it. I don't recall ever knowing what suicide was as a kid. All I know is I didn't want to be here anymore. After all the abuse that I endured, I just didn't know how to be alive anymore. When I used to hide in the closet under the clothes, I used to try and suffocate myself, so I could stop breathing. I couldn't do it long enough to finish it. I tried on numerous occasions, but I was never successful at it. I would always try to do what I knew, as I didn't know any other way but by suffocation. Since I couldn't do that very well, I stopped trying.

One day, I was sitting in my room just dazed and thinking, and out of nowhere I heard this voice say, "Kill yourself." I looked around, and no one was there. I thought I was tripping, but I had never heard this before. Just like I heard the voice say, "You like girls." I heard the voice say, "Kill yourself."

I know it wasn't me because I didn't say anything. But I did hear it, and I know I'm not the only one. People are killing themselves every day, and it's sad. They have no other escape, and when the enemy comes in and plant thoughts in the minds of people, suicide is the result of that.

See the enemy knows when to come in, just like God. When we're at our lowest point in life, that's when he decides to show up. This is the enemy's way of giving us an escape from our problems. But the Bible says endure:

James 1:12: God blesses those who patiently endures testing and temptation. Afterward, they will receive the crown of life that God has promised to those who love Him.

James 1:2-4: My brethren, count it all joy when you fall into various trials, knowing that the testing of your faith produces patience. But let patience have its perfect work, that you may be perfect and complete, lacking nothing.

Ephesians 6:10-18: Finally, my brethren, be strong in the Lord and in the power of His might. Put on the whole armor of God, that you may be able to stand against the wiles of the devil. For we do not wrestle against flesh and blood, but against principalities, against powers, against the rulers of the darkness of this age, against spiritual hosts of wickedness in the heavenly places. Therefore, take up the whole armor of God, that you may be able to withstand in the evil day, and having done all, to stand. Stand therefore, having girded your waist with truth, having put on the breastplate of righteousness, and having shod your feet with the preparation of the gospel of peace; above all, taking the shield of faith with which, you will be able to quench all the fiery darts of the wicked one. And take the helmet of salvation, and the sword of the Spirit, which is the word of God; praying always with all prayer and supplication in the Spirit, being watchful to this end with all perseverance and supplication for all the saints

If I had listened to the voice, I wouldn't be here today. I know I have a purpose to pursue. After that, I still felt like I wanted to die. But I don't recall ever trying to kill myself again. So, what did the enemy do? He tried to kill me. But he wanted me to see how it's done.

After leaving from school, I came home, and I was told that my mom tried to kill herself. I couldn't help but wonder if the same voice that told me to kill myself was the same voice that told my mom to kill herself. Life was so hard for my mom, and I understood why she no longer wanted to be here. But to try and kill herself would be hard to do. Specially to leave your kids here alone with people who don't really love them.

I was told that she took a combination of pills, but she was fine. My mom took every pill she could. Uppers, Downers, Xanax, and Valium. Who knows what else, she had all kinds of pills around. I wondered if anyone, besides me, cared about my mom. Why wasn't she committed to the state hospital or something? The hospital was supposed to recommend that, right? Or so I thought. Maybe it wasn't like that back then. That wasn't the last time it happened, either. As a matter of fact, Big Joe use to threaten her. He would say "I will have you're a** committed" and spend the check for turning you in. Then he would laugh about it.

The next time it happened, it was still daylight outside, it was nice, and everyone was outside playing including myself. I was still in elementary school when this happened. I just so happen to come around the corner toward our apartment. We were still living at The Forest Place, I happen to look up and I saw my mom hanging over the balcony on her back, crying her eyes out, screaming, and her hands were bloody. So, I ran upstairs to check on her, and I found that she had slit her wrist with a knife. I was more embarrassed than anything, but I felt bad for her, too. They took my mom in the house and cleaned her up. The Emergency Medical Service came, wrapped her wrist, this time they asked if she wanted to go to the hospital. The only reason she's still alive is because the knife was dull, and she didn't hit the main artery.

I was just shocked that she was trying to kill herself and no one saw anything wrong with it. She tried what she knew, and it wasn't working. I was wondering why there was no help for suicidal people or maybe that was not a big deal back then. I didn't know what to say, but I thought about the voice again. That same voice that was talking to me was the same voice talking to my mom. I know as a kid, I use to hear Big Joe threaten my mom sometimes saying. If you don't stop tripping I will have you locked up. He told her this on numerous occasions. He never did it, he just made the threats. He was to selfish to lock her up. That means she wouldn't be around for him to play with. And he would have to keep all of his kids all day every day. I'm sure he was not capable of doing that.

To me, it was an example of what the enemy wanted me to do. If I saw my mom doing it, maybe it was okay to try and do it to myself. But I didn't want to try suicide anymore; I just wanted to be left alone. The different voices that kept coming to me made me have to fight in my mind. I stayed mentally drained all the time, almost to the point of a breakdown. Most of my days were spent alone with reoccurring daydreams, and a lot of fantasizing about a life spent away from here. I was constantly telling this voice no and to go away.

Today, I tell people I should be in the state hospital somewhere staring at a wall, out of my mind. Now that I think about it, my mom and I should be in the same room because it seems that she may have been going through some of the things I was dealing with. After seeing that, I didn't know what to think; the one thing I knew for sure was that suicide was not for me. My mom kept trying, and it didn't work.

I was still in elementary school and we were living with Uncle Taft still at the Forest Place Apartments. My mom's ex-boyfriend Dean showed up. He'd gotten out of jail and was looking for her. He came and knocked on my uncle's door, and she went outside in the hallway. At that time, the hallway had doors to them, so no one could see in unless they walked up to the two side windows. I went outside with my mom in the hallway because I didn't trust him. (I will go into more detail about this story in a later chapter).

Let's just say this guy was looking to make her pay. They were in the hallway fussing and then fighting. I was in the middle trying to keep him from hurting my mom. He pulled out a gun like he wanted to kill her. She was holding his hand; I was holding his hand up in the air, screaming, and crying. And the gun went off. I don't remember what happened after that, but at the time, I felt so afraid for my mom and me.

I initially forgot about the incident. As I got older, I would have this reoccurring dream about being in that same hallway sitting on the ground with blood running down the side of my head. I could literally feel the heat from the blood that rolled down the side of my face and onto my shoulder. But I would always see the guy we fought with at high school. I couldn't pinpoint what it meant. I guess because we were beefing so tough with this guy that it reminded me of that incident. It didn't help that people were getting killed in our group, or shall I say in our gang. I've heard people say, once something traumatic happens, it's something victims want to forget, especially as a kid. If we don't get help, it stays hidden until we're able to deal with it.

There were a few times we would come home and see things that kids shouldn't see. I believe I was in middle school at the time of one incident.

After being in school all day, we just want to go home and relax. On this particular day, we came home from school and looked down the sidewalk and saw people standing around, so we went looking to be nosy. A man was lying on the ground, dead. It didn't look as if he was bloody, but he was dead. Everyone stood around watching him. He was out in the open in the middle of the cuts. That is what we called the area of the apartments where everyone hung out. Where we lived, all we had to do was stand downstairs and look down the sidewalk, and we could see everything that was happening. I have no idea how long he was there or where the police and the ambulance were. They finally came, but it seemed like forever before they got there to pronounce him dead. He wasn't covered up or anything, just lying there dead in the open in front of everyone.

This was almost a regular thing where we grew up. We saw another dead body. This time everyone was talking about it. We had to actually go around the corner to see this one. It was me my brother Ray, Tay and a few friends. We started walking down the sidewalk from our apartment, we made a left and then a right. We knew the dead guy, and we knew the guy who had supposedly killed him. We went to look for ourselves. He was lying in his front door like he was running in the apartment when he had been shot several times. Blood was everywhere, and he was lying face down, dead. I began to see death all around me; it was crazy in those apartments. I know for sure we weren't the only ones seeing stuff like this. But again no one was talking about it.

When I say the enemy tried to kill me, he did. Over a period of time, little incidents began to happen to me. The first one was when we lived in The Forest Place Apartments. This was when the gangs were getting started. Some of the older guys were hanging out, and we were out there just hanging around and being kids. Some guys came out in the apartments. I believe they were from a rival gang; they began shooting at the older guys we knew, and we all took off running.

One of the young guys Pop and I were running together in the same direction. Trying to get home and out of harm's way. We turned one of the corners and ran right into one of the shooters. We stopped in our tracks as the barrel of his gun was pointed right in our faces. We were so scared we didn't even see what he looked like. All we saw was gun. Thank God, he was not trigger happy and realized we were two kids running from the sound of bullets. He just let us go, and we took off running again in the other direction. I had never been so scared in my life. I thought I would die that day.

Another time, I was living in a different apartment complex called Montego Place and I was about eighteen years old. Another incident happened while I was hanging out with Bill, one of my guy friends, in his neighborhood called The Spot. We were standing around talking and having a good time. Some guys from a rival gang came by and started shooting. We hit the ground, hiding behind cars and buildings. I scarred up my hand and knees on the concrete. He kept apologizing to me on the way home. After that night I vowed I would never go back again.

There were a few incidents that happened in the Montego Place Apartments, where rival gangs would come and shoot up the place. But no one died out there. We were sixteen, seventeen, and some eighteen; but we were in high school, going to visit our friends in the hospital who had been shot multiple times because someone was bold enough to walk up to the door and shoot into their apartment. We were too young to be seeing that kind of stuff.

As a result, when someone would tell me they had a hard life, I say tell me if it sounds like mine. When someone judge us for how we use to act, find out what our eyes have seen and what our minds may be still holding. I wouldn't judge a book by its cover without really reading the pages for myself. And I still try to find out people's story before I make assumptions about them. The good stuff is on the inside. Please don't judge us by our past, it's merely a reaction to the environment we grew up in. Good people come out of the hood too. We were merely trying to make it in life like everyone else. Our route was just a little different. For everyone who judged us, all you had to do was meet us where we were, at that time. Trying to control someone doesn't work.

I have been kidnapped twice, raped once and almost thrown out of a moving car on the highway. I've had a gun pulled on me, which I will go more into detail in a later chapter. The scary thing is I wasn't afraid to die. I figured if I didn't have to do it myself, maybe someone else would be more successful at it. Because so much has happened to me, I was tired before I was twenty-one years old. I couldn't help but think this couldn't be all that life had to offer. But because of the grace of God, I kept fighting.

> *Romans 8:38-39: And I am convinced that nothing can ever separate us from God's love. Neither death nor life, neither angels nor demons, neither our fears for today nor our worries about tomorrow-not even the powers of hell can separate us from God's love. No power in the sky above or in the earth below-indeed, nothing in all creation will ever be able to separate us from the love of God that is revealed in Christ Jesus our Lord.*

> *John 10:10: The thief does not come except to steal, and to kill, and to destroy. I have come that they may have life and that they may have it more abundantly.*

I renounce all thoughts of suicide that may run rampant in my mind and in my thoughts in the name of Jesus!

I break all curses of suicide that may have passed down from one generation to the next in the name of Jesus!

WHO TOLD YOU THAT YOU WERE A DOORMAT?
(Physical and Mental Abuse)

At times, I wonder if men are aware that women are not put on this earth to be beaten up. God placed us beside man as a helpmeet. We help a man in his vision for his life and the life of his family. I am convinced that the men in my mother's life did not know this. If they did, they didn't care. As previously stated, they loved her, but it was superficial. Once they showed her that they didn't have her back and weren't in her corner. She didn't want to have anything to do with them and she lost respect for them.

I learned that very early on. I watched how man after man came and went in and out of my mom's life. A few stayed around but they didn't last because she didn't want them. When I said the men loved my mom, they did. They loved what she could do for them and she knew it.

My mom may not have said it, but I knew, and I watched her. I'm more like my mom in so many ways. After I see I can't trust a person or that they don't really care about me, I can't mess with them. I can forgive them, but the relationship will never be the same. It defeats the purpose of being in a relationship with that person.

The only person my mom Shae ever loved was Big Joe. Once Big Joe showed her that he didn't care enough to stay around, she didn't care about anyone after that. True enough, every time he came back and whispered sweet nothings in her ear, she took him back. She would drop everyone else like a bad habit. This resulted in the same thing; he only stayed around for a little while. He would always tell her he would marry her but never did. Matter of fact, he got married twice but not to her. She had a ring and everything. She never took the ring off; she held on to that promise for dear life, but it never changed anything. My mom had kids by Big Joe, and she was considered the other woman. It was so sad because my mom had at least two men who I remember really cared about her and her kids. But they were not who she wanted.

There was Dean, he was one of the few that actually lived with us. My mom was actually in a relationship with him until it went south. He lived with us in the Algonquin Apartments. At the time I was in elementary school. He may be one of the reasons why we were evicted, but as I said before, we had so much going on in the apartment, it could have been a number of reasons. He was an okay dude; he never hurt us. At least I don't recall if he did. He tried to help, but he had a bad attitude. Kam and Ray was still living with us at the time. Uncle Taft had his own apartment at the Forest Place but was over visiting.

This was around the time my mom was no longer going out on jobs. She had a man and no longer needed to go. We didn't have a house full of people because he put a stop to that. As I recall there was no more partying either. There was a man in the house now. Dean tried to domesticate her as much as he could. I believe it may have been a Sunday because she had cooked and everything. My mom, uncle Taft and I walked to the neighborhood store across the tracks. We were on our way to the local grocery store Andersons. Before we could get to the store, my mom's boyfriend Dean showed up. He was tripping over something unimportant and I was too young to remember what it was about.

Again, I believe he was trying to control my mom and couldn't. So, whatever he was tripping about wasn't that serious to walk and come and look for my mom. He could have waited until we got back from the store. If I say he beat my mom like she was a dude because, of course, my mom was not going to let him talk crazy to her. My uncle Taft couldn't help because he was on a cane, and I think he was already afraid of him. So, all he did was scream at him and tell him to stop. I was screaming and crying saying, "leave my mom alone." Anyone who has ever walked over the tracks knows there are humungous rocks on the trail. She fell on the rocks, and he kicked her and beat her some more. I don't even remember what happened after that or how she got to the hospital. I was traumatized by what I just saw. I just know he took off, and we couldn't find him. The police took pictures and filed a police report.

My mom's lips, knees, and hands were busted up, and she had two black eyes and a crushed spirit. The story my mom told, and she stuck to it, was Kam started all that mess. Kam was supposed to have told Dean something about mom that pissed him off, and he came after her in anger and revenge. Mom said Kam was evil like that and couldn't be trusted. It was serious because Kam moved out after that. I was told something different from Kam.

I asked her, "Why did you move out," and she said, "I was tired of all her boyfriends."

I didn't know what to believe, so I stopped asking because everyone in my family acted like they didn't know how to tell the truth anyway. That's why I chose not to deal with them; they never told the truth, which made things worse for all of us. They were obviously secret keepers too.

Seeing my mom get beaten up by a man for the first time was traumatic for me. That is where some of the fear came from. I didn't feel like I could trust anyone. I tried to stay sane, but so much of the stuff I saw kept replaying in my head. I felt like I didn't have a voice, so that turned me into an introvert. All my emotions were spent on crying as a kid, which later led to the anger that I harbored. I would talk so much trash under my breath in order for me to feel like I fought back. I just wanted someone to please come and get me out of this family and this life. Didn't anyone see what was going on, or did they just not care? I couldn't help but think this was not normal nor was it healthy for a kid to live like this. And after a while, I would fantasize about being somewhere else.

I had made up in my mind that I would have my own escape. Besides reading all those books, I would think about other things. I would think about life outside of this place. I would go somewhere in my mind and stay there and not come back. I just wanted out. We didn't go right back to the apartment after my mom got out of the hospital. When we did go back, that is when we were evicted. All of our belongings were sitting outside in the open. That is how we ended up at uncle Taft's apartment. We were hiding out from Dean.

When my mom left, she found out dean was looking for her. Once he got out of jail, he came right to my uncle's and that is why there was a fight in the hallway with the gun incident. We never knew how he found her so quickly. But who knows, people talk so much. My uncle may have told, everyone knew just give Uncle Taft a drink and he will tell everything. My mom was killing the men softly. She was not letting up on these dudes. It's only because they didn't know what to do with her. If they had stopped trying to control her, they could have kept her.

After that incident happened in the hallway, we never saw him again. I don't know if my mom did or not, but we didn't. Once we finally got our own apartment in the same complex as uncle Taft. That's when Big Joe started showing back up. He would come back and forth whenever he felt like he could get away with it. Kam started coming on the weekends. Like I said before, it wasn't any better, just a different place, same faces. My uncles were always there like wolves waiting to eat the sheep. I grew up around a bunch of pedophiles. If I could see them, why couldn't anyone else? All I had to do was look in their eyes. That scared me, too, because I could see them for who they really were.

Kids shouldn't have to deal with those types of issues. I could see the spirit on them. I didn't know what it was back then; I just knew it scared me. I just tried to stay away from them as much as

I could. It was like they were waiting around to get me alone. I had to make sure I was never alone in the apartment with any of them.

I couldn't have sleepovers because of that reason. I was too afraid the same thing would happen to my friends. I didn't want that for any of them. One year, I was going to have a slumber party for my birthday. It got canceled because of that reason. All these men were hanging around. I couldn't help but think, why were they here? They needed to go and do something with themselves.

I found out later that my uncles PJ, Pete and Taft were at our apartment for my mom too. I couldn't tell if Big Joe kept coming around because he was in love with her or because he didn't want his brothers and uncles to have her. They all used her up, so no one was innocent in that situation. I just hate that she never came to herself.

One thing my mom didn't give up was her drinking. Once she awoke in the morning she was off to the store to get beer. Either that or her friends would come early and bring some with them. I think she slowed down on the pills, though. At least I couldn't tell if she was on them anymore. At this moment we were living at the Forest Place Apartments. I have no idea what happened or why it did, but my mom and Big Joe were arguing, and it was loud. I walked in the living room, and Big Joe was beating up my mom. My brothers and I were screaming for him to stop. He got mad and cursed us out. But I was standing there watching him beat up my mom? How did he think we were supposed to act? We were mad, scared, and upset. He was no better than any other man on the street, if he allowed his kids to watch him hit their mom. We know longer had any respect for him. And this is the man she wanted to marry. Wow!!

This wasn't the last time he hit her, either. He would always call mom out of her name. After a while, she didn't look like herself anymore. She was no longer the pretty lady I remembered. Her skin got dark, and teeth were missing. Mom was so beat up by life and men that she no longer cared to be alive anymore. I'm sure that's why the suicidal thoughts began to show up. They were trying to give her a way out. All because these men couldn't control her. They had to try and slow her down any way they could. That's why we have to be careful with our thought life. Whatever we babysit in our minds, it will manifest some way.

Everyone in the hood thought we were lucky because they saw Big Joe come around. Some of them had never seen their dads, so I know why they would think like that. But they had no idea what happened behind closed doors. Everyone just thought my mom was crazy, but no one ever asked why she acted like she did. What people don't know is when Big Joe came around it was just to punk us. He tried to control everything we did. We were so emotionally unattached. We had no clue on how to express ourselves. My oldest brother Ray would get upset and beat his head against the wall. Once that was over, he would sit and rock until he couldn't anymore. That is what people don't see. He called everyone in the house an *'effin dummy*.

My mom is not the only one Big Joe hit. He also hit Kam for mouthing off, he busted her lip. That fear I felt changed that day,

I went into survival mode. I thought I would be next. But he never hit me.

On a Friday evening Kam came over our house for the weekend. Like she usually does, and we were playing around outside, and I noticed she had bruises all over her arms. I asked her what happened. All she said was nothing. I respected her choice not to speak on it. We went on about our business. Big Joe never hit me like he hit them. I've seen more as a kid than any one person has seen in a lifetime. That's when I made a vow that I later had to ask for repentance for. If he had ever hit me, I was going to kill him. I would replay in my head until it manifested on my face. And I made sure he knew that I didn't like him. When he looked at me, he could see that in my eyes. I would always say to myself, "If you touch me I will kill you." I would say this repeatedly. Every time I would see Big Joe put his hands on someone in the apartment, I would immediately go into my mind and repeat it. *Touch me if you want to, I will kill you.*

I have done some stuff to make him want to hit me. Why? Because I knew he and Big Mama tried to control my mom, and they tried to control me, too. He has never whooped me or hit me. I don't know if it's because of what my face said or if he was too afraid I would tell everyone what he did.

Big Joe did try to be there when we went on trips to my mom Shae's hometown. We pretended as if we were a family by dressing alike and everything. The damage was already done, and there was no turning back from that. In this situation the bad outweighed the good in my opinion. Our perception of family was so wrong. There was one time I tried to give Big Joe another chance.

I was living with Jewel, one of my friends for a little while. He came to visit and took us out for a while; my friends and me. I thought to myself, okay he may be trying again. I decided to give him a chance. Well he takes us to the store and then expressed that I shouldn't tell Kam. I asked, "Why not." He says, "she will be mad."

She will be mad? I thought, well what about me? I was thinking what kind of wicked stuff do y'all have going on over there, "You know I'm your daughter too right?" But I calmed down and answered my own question. No, I'm not because you don't even know me. He did buy us stuff at the store and took us to eat. But he was not over there for me. He was trying to talk to my friend. That is why I never bought females around. They were all wolves in sheep's clothing, even Big Joe.

Until people in my family make Big Joe own up to some of the stuff he has done, we probably will never have a real relationship. I'm okay with that because forgiveness and repentance are the roads I have chosen. I give all the honor and glory to God for that. My mind was a mess, and I'm just now being okay with some of the stuff I've seen and heard. Every time I write a part of this book, it has brought deliverance and healing for me. There are so many things I chose not to remember, but they have come back to me as I've been writing. There were conversations me and Big Joe had that made me question whether he knew I was his daughter or not. The conversations made me very uncomfortable. I couldn't wait to get away from him.

The result of seeing my mom being beaten up by men caused me to become the controlling one in a relationship; that is why I have tried to stay away from relationships. I knew I had issues. I should have given a disclaimer, "If you mess with me, I will mess your whole life up!" I would only get in relationships if I could control them. Anyone who had any authority in their voice, I stayed away from them because I thought they would try to control me. The fear would rise up in me and I would run. Even though a part of me wants a real relationship bad. It's just so hard for me. I don't have a problem with a stern man, as long as he knows who I am. Otherwise, there comes the fight.

Even today, I have some fear that I won't be able to have a healthy relationship because of my past. I thought I was damaged goods, so I would have to take the next best thing. A cute face and cute shape just don't do it. If we have inner issues, eventually, those issues come out.

One of my relationships kind of got out of hand. Enoch was probably the second man I had been in a relationship with. I wouldn't count the first one, that was considered puppy love.

Even though I had a baby, I didn't really know what I was doing. I like to call it just practicing for the real thing. Let's just say it lasted about two years, which was usually my limit in everything until it began to get rocky. Two years was all a man would get from me. But this one wasn't my fault. I found out Enoch was snorting powder, and he was turning into this ugly beast. I was like ugh, nope, can't do this. I found out he cheated on me with some basic chick. I said, "Dude, you're not even all that. How are you going to treat me like I'm a scrub? I'm doing you a favor by messing with you."

That's crazy because I didn't have any esteem, but I knew I was way better than half these chicks out here. I told this fool I didn't want to mess with him anymore. He bought me stuff and tried to make me feel bad. Nope, I was tired of being with him, anyway. Like I said before, two years was my max.

When I found out he cheated, I was like okay. I got me a friend, and he found out. One of the chicks in the apartment, who didn't like us, told him that I was gone with some dude. This fool began stalking and following me everywhere I went. I had to move in with Big Mama, so that he couldn't find me, but he did.

This was a normal week day and I walked my daughter to the neighborhood elementary school she was going to. This fool showed up and chased me down early in the morning. He kidnapped me. I was running down the street trying to get away from him; he made me get in the car with him. Once we got to an apartment, I have no idea who lived there. He pushed me in the room. With the gun to my head, he made me have sex with him. It's crazy, but I wasn't afraid of the gun being placed to my head. I didn't care because I wasn't afraid to die. But he later brought me home. All the while, I was still messing with my new friend.

I wouldn't answer his calls or see him in any kind of way.

Maybe a month or two later, my friends and I went to the neighborhood nightclub called Rhapsody. I was only in there a few minutes. He was obviously following me because he showed up, grabbed my neck, and made me leave with him. We were in the car fighting, and he tried to push me out of the car on the highway. We were trying to stay on the highway driving and swerving, licks being thrown, slapping, and kicking. After some convincing, he finally took me back to my friend's house.

Another time when it happened, we were at a different nightclub on San Juan City Base. He showed up there also, grabbed my neck, kidnapped me, and made me have sex with him again. I just wanted this fool to leave me alone. I couldn't go anywhere without him showing up.

The last incident happened when I was meeting my new friend Jay T at his cousin Meme's apartment. His cousin and I were friends first. That is how I met him. There was a knock on the door. I went to let him in, and he told me my friend Enoch was outside. He was standing right behind him. He had been watching me the whole time; he grabbed me out the apartment. And there we went, fighting in the apartments. Someone heard us scuffling and called the police.

After I talked to the police that night, I went back to my friend Meme's apartment, and her cousin was still there. I had to tell Jay T what happened. He was like do I need to get involved? I told him, no, he's going to jail. And this is my issue and I don't want to get you involved in my mess. I wanted him to leave me alone. It was hard trying to move around with someone following me all the time and showing up out of nowhere. I had to get a restraining order on him. The next morning Big Joe took me downtown to try and get one. I was told he is already locked-up and they couldn't serve him until he got out. The cops were already looking for him for other stuff, anyway, so that helped me out a lot. They kept him locked up.

Sometimes people look at me and say that I look mean. It's not that; I just have this face that says not to approach me until I check you out first. I really am a nice person. I have learned to screen people first before I get too close. But I give everyone a chance, no matter what other people may say about them. I have to find out on my own who you really are, only because I know what it feels like to be judged based on your past or based on someone else's opinion. I never had a chance with my family. They abused me and then treated me like I was my mother. They thought I was going to end up like her. But that was not God's plan for me.

Isaiah 53:5: But he was wounded for our transgressions, He was bruised for our iniquities; The chastisement of our peace was upon Him, and with His stripes we are healed.

WHO TOLD YOU THAT YOU WERE A THIEF?

When I was a thief, I stole everything I could get my hands on. I didn't realize how bad it was until I got older. We did crazy stuff, but I needed an escape, and, at the time, that was it for me. That was my way of acting out and being rebellious. No one could tell me anything. If anyone tried to tell me anything, I wouldn't listen. My saying was, "You can't tell me anything because your life isn't right, either." Again, I didn't think anyone wanted me to tell on them if they said anything about me or to me.

I would steal anything; I think that was a way of having control over something in my life. I didn't have any control over the abuse, so I needed to have some kind of control. I started off stealing stuff out of people's houses. My mom had this friend name Patty who had a daughter whose name was Jolee. We became best friends immediately. Her mom let me get behind the wheel of the car and try to drive. I couldn't help but think, *Wow, she's cool.* My mom never learned to drive, so she couldn't teach me. My new friend was cool, too.

We learned new stuff from each other like new ways to steal. Yes, I found out she was a thief, too, and we hung out together all the time. We would go to the neighborhood store and steal. We would walk in the store, get a brown paper bag, walk around the other side of the cash registers, fill up the bags with candy, and walk out the store like we paid for it. That was too easy for me, though. I needed something else, but it worked for a little while.

It was short and sweet because they only stayed around for a little while. They would come back every now and then but never stayed long. Or her mom would come without her. It seems that I had to find another friend.

And I did, I began hanging out with the boys. Mostly, my brother Ray and his friends. That's when me and Rat became best friends. We thought we liked each other but that didn't last long at all. We were too much alike and we knew that. Even though I let him put hickeys on my neck. We knew we were the same person. It wasn't going to work anyway. When my mom saw the hickeys, I got a whooping for having them and then sent back outside to play.

The boys and I would do crazy stuff like play "left hand give it up" in the store with stuff we hadn't paid for and walk out like it was ours. I got caught one time, I was in the store alone because I needed something for my hair. I went to get hair gel from the neighborhood store Andersons. I got caught and had to call my mom to come get me. She came to get me, and that was it. Mr. Anderson knew my mom, so he did not trip out too bad. Of course, I was sure it was because he liked her, they all did. If I knew then what I know now, I wouldn't have stolen from him mainly because he was an African American business owner trying to have something for us in the hood. We weren't thinking about that, especially if no one is teaching you about it.

Sometimes in high school, one of my very best friends Tonie and I used to steal all the time. She was truly my stealing buddy. We never had to explain that to each other, we just went in and did it. When we had a pep rally at school or a program in the auditorium, we would go to the big grocery store Shmee'go on

Calgon Rd before school and steal snacks. We would load up our backpacks; the snacks kept us from falling to sleep while the program was going on. We would be in there passing out snacks like crazy. We never thought anything about it; we just did it because it was easy.

Tonie lived in the Forest Place Apartments on the other end of our building. She had stuff going on in her apartment too. But she was very intelligent, as a matter of fact, all of her sisters were very smart. Their mom Bernie on the other hand, everyone called crazy. The story everyone talks about was when Bernie and our downstairs neighbor Cora had a fight over this man. He was married to Cora but messing with Bernie. The fight ended with Cora sliced and bleeding and Bernie nowhere to be found. That was when everyone called her crazy.

One evening Tonie and her mom Bernie got into a fight and she ran away to my house. I hid her and let her stay there for a couple of hours. Bernie came looking for her. She came to my apartment and called Toni's name. I told her that she was not with me. Bernie got mad cause she already knew she was with me. Toni finally came out and Bernie beat the mess out of her before she got to the apartment. Before she walked away she told me, "don't you ever keep my child from me."

Tonie and I would also go downtown to the discount store serv-a-lot and steal clothes. We would take two of what we wanted and try them on. One item we would try on and leave on under our clothes we wore in the store, the other we would take out and hang it back up. We would leave out the store with a whole outfit under our clothes. It was just too easy for us, so we did it.

I stole from everyone; no one was exempt. I stole from school. I stole from the classrooms. I didn't care about getting in trouble or about hurting anyone. All I cared about was myself. As I got older, I began to connect with other thieves. No one was afraid to steal. That was just how it went in the hood; we didn't have time to be scary. Then the new thing was to do a "clothes run."

Annie had done the clothes run before and said we could go with her. Annie and I weren't friends, but she was friends with my friend Maddie. Pearl was also a friend of Maddie's who was friends with Annie. Pearl and I hung out before, she's cool but I wouldn't say were friends. I figured if Maddie and Pearl was okay with Annie then she could be trusted. We planned it and she explained what we had to do. She said go to the mall, choose a store that had an exit door to the street. Pick the clothes we wanted, then run out the store, jump in the car, and then we leave. We had planned to do the same stunt, but when we were on our way the situation with the car fell through. We tried another time, and the same thing happened; they couldn't get the car. I figured maybe we weren't supposed to do that. We were ready to go at any time, it just didn't happen for us.

While in high school, my friends and I from the Forest Place Apartments, were beefing with this guy name Ed who didn't like us. All because of the guys we hung out with. I had a fight with this Ed in the principal's office. This was an on-going beef with him. We were so mad at him that me, Jewel and Tonie left school one day and broke into his house. We went through his bedroom window and took jewelry and any athletic apparel he had. Some people may ask, "Why you didn't take more stuff and sell it? If you get caught, why not get caught for something worth taking?"

Well, because we were only mad at him and not his mom or his sisters, so we only took his stuff. We wore his clothes to school like they were ours; we didn't have any shame, either. We didn't think about it at the time, but we could have gone to jail for breaking into someone's house. That's how warped our thinking was.

I never thought about who I was hurting at that time; I was selfish and unconcerned with any and everyone else. Once I had my daughter, a few things changed but not much. I was still a thief, and it was her first birthday. I didn't have any money to have her a birthday party. So, what did my friends and I do? Of course, we stole everything. A few of my friends and I went to the same neighborhood store. Mind you, we were now adults and should have known better. It was cold outside, so we had on these big jackets. We first went to Andersons, the neighborhood store and stole candy, candy bags, balloons, decorations, and party favors. The only thing we paid for was the hot dogs and the buns. That's because we couldn't fit those in the jackets.

Since we needed more for the party, we had a guy Mateo from the Forest Place Apartments, who tweeked on occasion, take us to the store to get the big stuff. All we had to do was get his baby some Pampers and that was payment for taking us. We went to the nearest grocery store Shmee'gos on Calgon Road. We picked up a cake had them write on it, put it in the basket along with two gallons of juice, three packs of Pampers, one for my baby, Mateo's baby, and my friend Addy's baby. We also got a big tub of ice cream with the handle, rolled out the store like we paid for it all and went home. The only thing we paid for was the mylar balloons. We just act like we paid for the items in the back. The next day, my baby had her first birthday party and at Addy's apartment and enjoyed herself. We never thought anything about it. That was just our survival mode, and it was like that for a while.

I finally moved into my own place in the San Juana Apartments. I was working for a temp service from Virginia Beach. I was able to get the job because I went to the trade school. I was making more money than everyone around me. I finally had my own sanctuary for a while. I still had the same mindset, though. I needed stuff for my apartment, so if I went to the store, I would pick some stuff up. When I went to the grocery store, I paid for the stuff I needed and grabbed a plant, or a trash can because they would set them outside. I had a receipt in my hand but not for those particular items. I would just grab them on the way out.

My friend Addy worked at one of the General Stores that sold everything. School was about to start for our kids. She told us to come get some stuff for the kids. All we had to do was go inside the store, get a bucket or a tub with a lid, fill it up with stuff, and just pay for the bucket only. We got clothes, socks, underwear, school supplies, and uniforms, we got all that we needed.

It didn't stop there, either. In 1998, I worked for this company called IBEW where I had to take inbound calls, and people gave me their credit card numbers. So, what did I do? That was the next come up for my friends and me. When someone would call in and order I would keep their credit card numbers and go shopping. I never used the same card twice, and because I had people calling from every city and state, they couldn't track or trace it. It was too easy for me. I paid our light and water bills over the phone. They figured it was my parents or someone in my family paying the bill. Most of the time it was an automated line. My friends and I went to concerts and comedy shows. We ordered clothes, shoes, and stuff for our apartments. I would get my friends their own card numbers, so they could do what they wanted to do with it.

One Christmas, although I had a job, it wasn't enough money to pay our bills and buy stuff for Christmas. We had Christmas at Addy's house because her place was bigger, and we could all fit. I got some more credit card numbers, and we ordered all the kids something for Christmas. We bought stuff for about twenty kids, and the tree was so full. The kids were excited. All the kids had about five or six presents apiece. It was so easy because, around that time, everyone was ordering stuff and delivering to family in other states. That went on for a while and it worked, it got old, but we did it until I was no longer working there. I apologize to anyone who was a victim of that situation. I wasn't thinking of the consequences, and I wouldn't want that to happen to me.

At some point in 2000, I received my housing voucher. I finally found a house, and before I moved, I went to a nearby furniture rental place. I picked out some new furniture, which included a big screen television with a wall unit, coffee table, end tables, a refrigerator, washer, and dryer. I paid the first payment to get these items out the door. They delivered them to the San Juana Apartments. Then I moved a few weeks later. I never made another payment. It's just what we were doing at the time. A lot of people did it. The only thing I ask of God is to please don't let this happen to me when I get my business. I was not in my right mind; I was young. It was wrong, but that was just the mindset of our environment. That was considered our survival method. If I knew better, I would have done better.

Later, I linked up with this guy MJ, he lived in the San Juana Apartments. He was friends with my brother Tay. He worked at this big toy store down the street from our apartment. Mike was telling us about how we could get in and get out if we wanted to rob the place. It didn't matter to me. We talked about it and had a plan, but we could never pick the right time. It never happened, so I guess it was one of those things that was not in the plans for my life. That is just the way our minds were wired. I think we had too much time on our hands because I wasn't working, and we were doing drugs, too. So that may not have been a good idea, anyway.

I break all generational curses of poverty in the name of Jesus!
I renounce all forms of theft and stealing in the name of Jesus!
I break all curses on my finances from any ancestors that cheated or mishandled money in the name of Jesus!

Lord, teach me to profit, and lead me in the way I should go. (Isaiah 48:17 paraphrased)

Wealth and riches are in my house because I fear you and delight greatly in Your Commandments. (Psalm 112:1-3 paraphrased)

WHO TOLD YOU THAT YOU WERE A LIAR?

Being a liar is not very hard to do. A lot of people lie because it usually gets them what they want. I heard that it's okay to lie for your job when you're in sales. I found out that was not true; we shouldn't have to lie to get a sale. People can tell when a lie comes out of our mouths. Lying was never my thing. As a matter of fact, the only reason I began to lie was to get what I wanted. The other reason I lied was because people couldn't handle my truth. I was so brutally honest that I offended people. I would hear from people around me that I was mean, or that I didn't have to, "Say it like that."

After hearing it so much, it began to shape the way I thought about myself. That was one thing I knew for sure about myself—that I would tell the truth no matter what. Because I didn't have any self-esteem, anything people told me about myself, I thought they knew what was best for me. I would allow other people's opinion about me become believable in my own mind and my own esteem.

The tough part of that is I begin to wear what people put on me. Lying was a way to make me look and sound better than what I really was. My truth was taken from me because I didn't know who I was. This is because I had identity issues. For instance, I'm not really a fighter; I was made to fight by my siblings.

We were in the apartments on the weekend hanging out. Kam came and told me that this girl name Jade in the Forest Place Apartments was talking about my mom. If you knew me, you knew this was a very sensitive spot for me and Kam knew this. They made me walk up to the girl Jade and ask her about it. She didn't know what I was talking about. But I was told to hit her. I didn't give her a chance to explain herself. I just busted her in the face and didn't stop hitting her until they broke it up. I never forgot that girl and what we did to her. I always wondered why it always touched me and made me feel some type of way. Later, I realized it was because she didn't hit me back, and it reminded me of Big Joe beating up my mom and watching her in a helpless moment.

I don't like to fight; at least not in the natural. I wasn't scary, but I didn't like it, and there is a difference. I'm not built to fight in the natural, my mind is too strategic for it. I'm more of a fighter in the spirit. Where we come from, we had to fight. So that is what we did.

I never told anyone about that situation because I felt like they wouldn't understand, and I didn't want to look like a bully. I walked around like I was hard and made it seem like I was untouchable, only because not too many people would try me or my friends. We did, however, once we got to high school, began to do more fighting. Don't get me wrong, I am a tough person. I don't think it's very beneficial to play like I'm hard, especially if that's not who I really am. Because of where we grew up, we didn't have time to be humble or timid. I just took on the same mind set as my environment. We didn't like hanging with liars because we had people who would lie to our faces even when we knew the truth.

There was a time I had to lie about my mom working because I didn't want to be embarrassed in front of the other girls, whose moms were working women. My mom did work later on down the line but not at the time when the discussion was going on with the other girls. All she did was home health work. It wasn't much to make a difference in the household, but she tried something. She was worth more than that, though. She was smart and very gifted. I couldn't tell them my mom was on food stamps and getting a check from the state. That was not the thing to do for an already scarred identity. The only thing is that when I was telling them about her working, I didn't know where she worked, the phone number, or anything. They knew all this stuff about their mom's employment statuses.

I would always say to myself, *I will not be on food stamps or government assistance.* Being a liar was not a planned characteristic for me. Sometimes it would just come out like that because I didn't know who I was. As I got older, I would lie to men to get what I wanted so I wouldn't have to sleep with them. If I slept with them, I wouldn't take money from them. Like I said before that made me look too much like a prostitute. I've already been in that situation, and I didn't want to make a habit out of it.

As a parent, lying to our kids about doing something for them or coming to pick them up and then making them wait and never coming, breeds disappointment. It makes them feel like they're not good enough. Think about what we as parents are doing to our kids before we make the decision not to show up.

As a married woman, I tried my best to stay in it because I didn't want to be a part of the divorce statistic. I didn't want my kids to be hurt. I believed I hurt them more because the kids could see when I wasn't happy. I lived a lie for years in my marriage. I was done after the first six years, and I never said anything. There was a guy Manny, who was dating Annie a friend from church. They came and hung out with me and my husband Denny at the time. The next day I talked to Annie and she told me what Manny said. He told Annie that I wasn't into the relationship like Denny was. I was like he could see that, how? I made sure that when we were in public, I never disrespected him. I never let anyone else disrespect him, either. I then had to be truthful with myself. And admit I was done. He wasn't happy either and didn't know how to leave the marriage. Neither one of us wanted to be the one who left.

My eyes began to wonder and look at other men. I couldn't hide it anymore. I lied to myself because I didn't know how to leave. The truth is the marriage was a hiding place for me. I needed a covering and didn't have one. I don't regret the relationship. I regret staying in it too long.

As a result of me staying, I lied and cheated until I could no longer get away with it. I got tired of lying and wanted out. I allowed myself to get caught and used it as my excuse to disqualify myself from being in the marriage any longer. I did warn him before not to play me, or I would show him that I could be real sneaky, and I kept my word. When I said people couldn't handle my truth, they couldn't. That was my fault for allowing people to make me change what I believed about myself. People would ask me stuff, and I would tell them the truth. Then they would shy away because they didn't know what to do with it.

As a kid, I had to tell my friend Dee from The Forest Place apartments that she stank and smelled like a man. Everyone else thought I was mean, so maybe I could have said it another way. She was always hairy and manly looking than all of us. When she would get up off the concrete from sitting she would leave stains of sweat. To her credit I don't think she could help it. She wanted to spend a night over my house, but I had to tell her to take a shower first because she smelled fishy. I wasn't trying to hurt her feelings, I just didn't have anyone to teach me how to present my truth. That is how it comes out, offensive.

In one instance with two of my friends, I went to high school with. I found out that Jewel was kissing Diamond's boyfriend. I told Jewel, "I'm telling Diamond when I get a chance, because that is wrong." She thought I was playing. When I got home, I called Jewel and told her that Diamond was on the line and to tell her what happened. I made her explain this because I knew as friends, we shouldn't do that to each other. How about this same chick did everyone like that? Jewel did me the same way years later. But that wasn't how I rolled. I had to learn the hard way, and everyone around had to learn, too. That was a rule: we don't mess with the same guy as our friend. That is a truth I would never give up. If I knew something that could mess up our friendship, I would let my friend know first that I was telling. That was to give her time to tell on herself. I guess because I wasn't scared of anyone, I didn't care if someone was mad or not.

At the very beginning of my relationship with Enoch, I found out I was pregnant. I lied to him and I told him it was his baby, but it was actually Kojo's baby, my daughter's dad. We were still messing around every now and then. The reason I told Enoch it was his baby because I knew he had the money I needed for an abortion. The only reason I decided to have the abortion was because I was so worried about what Big Joe was going to think and say about me. At that time, I had already felt condemned by everything I did. I promise—they wouldn't allow me to be myself or make my own mistakes. To avoid the scrutiny, I chose to have an abortion. That was intense for me as a young adult; it just felt weird to me. It's hard to explain. It's almost like I knew that I was doing something wrong, but I believe I was given the okay to do it. It was like God gave me a pardon on this situation. I thank God I've never had to do it again. The only reason I knew about the abortion was when Big Joe wanted me to abort my daughter Tane.' So, he was the one who introduced abortion to me.

I knew I wanted more for myself, it was just so hard getting there. Especially with no support or positive reinforcements around me. I didn't want to be a statistic, two babies on the bus, one walking, and the other in the carrier. I didn't want to be that chick. I was only nineteen at the time. I had more time to grow. That also helped with making my decision to abort my second pregnancy.

I used to sell drugs. I'm not very proud of it, but I did. That's just what we did at the time. But one of my guy friends showed me how to cut it and how to make my money off it. So, what did I do? I sold my drugs and my boyfriend Enoch's drugs at the same time. I would pinch off of his stuff to make my money. I lied to him about it because he was always high or drunk, so he didn't know the difference. It caused us to fight, but I didn't care. He didn't scare me one bit. It was my way of getting back at him for cheating on me.

There was another situation with one of my friends Maddie. I had to tell her that her kids daddy smoked crack. She couldn't receive it at first, but she came back and asked me how I knew. I told her that he set up a buy for me and never came back. When I asked him about it, he didn't know what to say. She asked me, "How do you know he didn't just take the money?"

I replied, "First of all, I wouldn't lie to you about something like this. That is not a rumor you want to start."

I told her I was able to tell that he got me for the drugs and not the money. I just knew he smoked it because he couldn't make any money off the amount of sale it was. In order for him to make a sale off the drugs, it would have to be a bigger amount, so he could get something out of it. That's how the game goes. Maddie later found out I was telling the truth. She thanked me for being honest with her and for being her friend. The truth always prevails.

Once I begin going to church, I would do the same thing, standing in my truth no matter what. I didn't want to be a part of any mess going on. When someone came to me with some mess or some gossip, I would let that person know. "Hey, such and such, they want to tell you something," or "They're talking about you over here. You may want to ask them about that."

That was my truth until I got sucked in to the mess and didn't realize that it was going on. I was so mad at myself. Gossiping about people was more hurtful than the actual situation that took place. It was ugly and caused people to shy away from the church. I stand by my truth no matter what people may say about me. I refuse to be a liar. My truth may save a life. I now know to tell the truth in love.

I repent for any lie I have ever told, Lord please forgive me and cleanse me from all unrighteousness.
I repent for gossiping about anyone even if I was just listening to it, Lord please forgive me.
Lord, give me a sound heart, which is the life of my flesh. Remove from my heart any evil or sinful attitude.

WHO TOLD YOU THAT YOU WERE A THUG?

I would always say I wasn't in a gang, I just hung with the guys I grew up with who were in a gang. But the activity we were around and into, said otherwise. My friends and I flocked to the gang because there was no other place to go. We felt like we were a part of something, especially me, I felt the sense that someone would always have my back. We bought up all the black permanent markers at the neighborhood store. We began tagging the hallways in the apartments and the bathrooms at school. Well, pretty much everywhere we went. There was this guy from New York that was living downstairs from us in the Forest Place Apartments.

His name was Kente' and he drew a design on my jeans with a permanent marker. The jeans had my name and the name of the gang going down each leg. It was cute at that time because we were just starting out. If it had been a few years later, it would have been a target on my back. Only because it told the police where I was from and the name of the gang.

My friends and I were at school getting into fights. We were in the 10th grade at the time when we had our first big fight in the cafeteria at breakfast. It turned into this big brawl. Daisy was the one who came and told us that she received a note in her locker from some girl, talking about her and Deese, her then boyfriend. The girl walked up to Daisy they had words and then there was the fight. We all jumped in, it turned into this big brawl. It went all downhill from there. Most of our fights were because of the guys we called our boyfriends. I notice that every fight I was in was never my own, but from jumping in for one of my friends.

One particular time, me and Jewel were standing in the hallway at school talking, and out of nowhere, we got jumped by a group of girls that we didn't even know we had beef with. We found out later that they were told to fight us. The story told was that it was because of Ed, he paid the girls to jump us. We had to fight about six girls and it was only two of us. Our other friends weren't around at that time. They caught us off guard. When we left school, my friend Jewel had to go to the hospital. She got hurt during the fight.

About nine months later, I was walking down the hall at school. My brother Ray ran up to me and said Jewel got knocked out by Ed. I was so mad and ran to the office to see what happened. Jewel and Shon were sitting down in the office waiting to talk to the principal. I asked what happened. Jewel started explaining and I asked her, "why this punk a** dude always such a problem to us." As I was saying that he walked out of the principal's office saying something smart, so I hit him and he hit me. And there was the fight again, Jewel and Shon jumped in, the cops had to stop the fight. I didn't care that the cops were in the office, I was just frustrated that he was always at the center of our drama. After all the drama was over, Officer Norman, one of the cops we were cool with, told me how to fight a guy without getting hurt.

About a month later, two of my other friends Diamond and KeKe had a fight with Ed too. They also jumped him, we were not in school at that time, so we missed the fight. We were told that they beat him under the table with some locks that they carried on their key chain. After a while, the drama with Ed slowed down. In my opinion, I believe he was in love with Jewel, I don't know if those two ever hooked up. But there was always drama with Ed, Jewel and Rat. Because Jewel and Rat were dating at that time, Ed couldn't have her. So, I believe he was mad and caused a lot of drama.

We still had beef with other people. It was so bad that one day at school, the principal called us all out of class, me and my friends. He told us we needed to come down to the office. Apparently, there was a threat made on our lives. He said there were girls coming up to the school after us with guns. We all knew that was not how high school was supposed to be. Everyone wants their high school years to be the best. Fun is what it's called; we should want to have the best high school experience. No, not us; that's not how it went. We had to watch our backs everywhere we went. It's supposed to be good memories.

We went to the little neighborhood store, Bentley's, and bought up all the little razors we could find. So everywhere we went – school dance, skating rink, club or football games—we stuck them in the bottom of our shoes until we got inside. We had to hide them from the metal detectors. We, or someone we knew, almost always fought, and it always turned into a big brawl.

We started hearing about girls getting sliced with razors, and the boys were being shot and killed. We were jumped at school, and it still didn't slow us down. Our friends were shot and had to go to the hospital. That didn't slow us down, either. We had multiple fights at school, and we started losing friends. They were starting to see that it was getting serious. Some of them didn't grow up like we did. They may have had issues, too, but they didn't grow up in the hood like we did.

Once the razors got old and they no longer carried them in the store, we would take locks from the lockers and carry them on our keychains. We carried the little gavel, used to knock out the glass to pull the fire alarm, as key chains for protection. If anyone wanted to attack us, they got the locks or the gavel. That's just how it was, we had to protect ourselves at all times. We had to ride around in packs of at least five people at a time.

My friends that grew up in homes didn't see as much as me and my friends from The Forest Place Apartments. We saw more than they did as far as death, abuse, and life itself. The school tried everything; they brought us and another group of girls together to try and make peace. The school even bought us lunch from outside the school. Of course, we sat and ate the food together, but we did not call a truce. We never became friends and we never fought them either. But we did fight other girls. We were fighting guys and girls. The police became our friends because they saw how many girls didn't like us. They felt bad for us. I think they realized we were good kids. We just hung around the wrong people. We still went to class, we had babies and had good grades. That was just the hand we were dealt and how we grew up. There were a few guys who were on our team, too, because our group kept dwindling down slowly. They wouldn't let anyone mess with us while we were at school. After a while, it was only a few of us left that were tough enough to keep fighting.

My friends and I would go to school with our Chuck Taylors on and our Jerseys, always ready to fight. We didn't have time to dress up and be cute. There was always some mess going on that we had to be aware of. San Juan Police Department got wind of the mess going on at the school and learned that we were a target. They came to the school and took our pictures and had us down as gang affiliation. This was done just in case we came up dead—they would know who we were. Some of us took the pictures, but a few said no and told the police to get permission from their parents first.

We thought it was cute, not realizing that they had us labeled. It's sad when I think about it because we were all so young and did all this stuff. One might ask, "Where were the adults during all this mess?"

Some of the people we had previously hung out with had parents that cared, and that's why they no longer hung out with us. Our parents were doing their own thing and not worried about us. A few of my friends ran away from home and were gone for days. They got in trouble for it, but that's the kind of stuff that was going on in our heads as teenagers. It was just so much we, as kids, had to deal with and with all the complaints the adults made. They never really knew how to reach us. A few people tried, though, especially at the school. We weren't bothered with making decisions about college or growing up. We were just trying to survive.

There was a plan through the summer program Youth to Adulthood that I worked with; they took a group of us that were stuck in the middle. Not really honor roll but made decent grades to pass, not athletic and not college bound. Me and Tonie was picked for the group. We stayed in trouble enough to get noticed by the administrators. They would meet with a few of kids, take us outside the school to show us different things besides the life we saw in the hood. They fed us lunch, took us to the dog shows, the jailhouse—just different things in life. I liked it because it showed us how to think differently. That only lasted for a little while, though.

It wasn't enough to keep us out of trouble, though. We were already in too deep. While sitting at the lunch table one day, we heard gunshots outside the lunch window. All you saw was kids running, everyone trying to get away from bullets. It appears that someone came up to the school and shot one of the guys we knew. He wasn't part of our crew, but we did talk to him. He was a cool dude, and we were glad he didn't die. They carried him inside the school and kept him there until the Emergency Medical Service came to get him. It was scary and crazy all at the same time. It was scary having a shooting at the school like that but not enough for us to stop, although it slowed us down a lot.

The news came to the school, and we were locked down because of the shooting. We had to wait for our parents to pick us up or catch a ride home with someone. There's no way this was supposed to happen at school. In my opinion, they should have never taken prayer out of the schools. They didn't realize what we had going on at home, therefore, school was considered to be a safe haven for some kids. Now school is just like every other place, dangerous.

If there was no prayer at home, we could expect it once we got to the school. But not anymore. Prayer does work just in case we forget. Taking prayer away from school gave room for the enemy to come in. Instead of taking it away, prayer should have been added to our everyday life. Prayer changes things. I'm a firm believer in that.

While in high school my friends and I have been jumped before, we have jumped people. It kind of shaped how we think about people. The adults just judged us and believed they had all the answers for us but didn't. One night in The Forest Place Apartments we were walking from the corner store, and out of the blue these guys came by shooting. My friend Dottie had buck shots in her back from running from bullets. She didn't have to go to the hospital. She said she was okay, but the shots were hot. She was bandaged up and we went on our way. Most of this happened to us before the age of eighteen.

Most of the mess we saw or participated in was now in the streets or the apartments where we lived. The one thing they could never say about us was that we didn't love our kids, even though we were young parents. Out of all the stuff we were in, we made sure our kids were protected from it. We made sure we were taking care of our kids no matter what. A lot of stuff they didn't see. I know it was contradictive to how we were, but we made our kids our first priority and everything else last.

We were living in The Forest Place Apartments for the second time, we moved out and came back. There was new management, so we were eligible to move back. We lived in the apartment by ourselves, and my mom lived with my uncle around the corner. Well, one night we all decided to go out. My brother Tay watched the kids because he wasn't old enough to go out. We went downtown with a few fellas from the neighborhood. There was one particular guy we hung out with name Top. I would always call him by his Government Name, because I didn't respect him. In my opinion, he was scary. He talked so much garbage like he was going to do something. He never did. I have never seen him do anything. We were cool, but I told some of the guys, "if you ever got into with anyone, don't take Top."

Anyway, we all went downtown to a club called On the Rocks. We arrived about 11:30 and we were on one side of the club and a few of the fellas were on the other side. We were in the club about an hour and a half and then we had to leave. Why? Because the scary cat has gotten into a fight with a rival gang. We left and went home back to our apartment, which is a straight shot from the club. Our apartment was in front of the main road. Anyone can drive down the street and see us standing outside. People use to say all the time, that they saw me standing outside my apartment. That was creepy to me. Anyway, we were all standing outside, some of us were downstairs and others were standing upstairs. Out of nowhere came the bullets. Those same dudes that Top got into a fight with did a drive by on our apartment.

I was so mad because my daughter was in the bed sleep. No one was hurt that night, but it could have turned out bad. When it was all said and done, we went looking for this fool and he was in my daughter's room hiding in the closet. I was so done with him. I told him, "Fool, get your butt out of my daughter's room now!" I stopped hanging out with him after that. He started all that mess and went and hid in the closet. Wow! I was tougher than him.

I sit and think about all the stuff we did and how rough we were, what we had to endure and how we lived. Some of us made it out alive, and for those who didn't, it's sad because we were so young. I believe we began to slow down when our peers started going to jail. We moved away from the apartments and began to grow up a little at a time.

I consider our generation behind because of how we grew up. We didn't take education or our future very serious, so now we are between the ages of forty and forty-five and just now realizing what our purpose is. We had a slow start because of the way we grew up and the mindset we had about life. We were not afraid of anything and lived for the moment. Running from bullets, and going to hospitals to visit half dead teenagers due to gunshot wounds. Carrying around razors to protect ourselves from getting jumped. That was not a way to grow up or live. We couldn't enjoy ourselves when we went out, because we had to constantly watch our back. This shouldn't be a way to live a teenage life for anyone. There are some things I wish I could change but not a whole lot. I know for sure I wouldn't change the people I grew up with. We lived and learned a lot together. I thank God for the protection he had over us.

MY PROCESS

The hard part is over, but the process was hell on wheels. I've always felt like I was poison – meaning anyone I came in contact with would eventually get hurt. This knowledge made me afraid to be in relationships with men. I had to realize that the enemy was using me to harm them. I just wanted help, and no one was able to help me the way I needed.

Once I was introduced to Christ that was it for me, I was good. It was hard at first because I had to give up a lot. While walking out a consecrated lifestyle, this is almost always a requirement. I had to make sure my hands were clean, and my heart was pure. I began going to church services and volunteering at church when they needed help. I read as many books as I possibly could to help me with my walk with Christ. I was really specific with the authors, though, they had to be credible in order for me to believe them.

The first half of my marriage was when I needed Christ the most, because I had so much baggage. I was angry and mean. I intentionally allowed God to change me on the inside first.

Because of the mess I had in me, I tried to be careful with how I treated people. I didn't want to hurt anyone else. The first time I heard of fasting, I didn't think anything of it. The church was doing a corporate fast. I didn't fully understand what it meant, so I also had to read up on that. The church announced we were going on a Daniel fast, which was simple for me. We came in agreement that God would reveal some things during the fast. I didn't understand what the purpose was if I didn't believe anything spiritually fell off me. We did that a few years in a row. What changed my life was when I did a complete fast with nothing but water.

I realized that my walk with God was different from everyone else's. I had to do what was necessary for me. And if I wanted God to do more, I had to turn my plate down. So that is what I did. I did a complete fast. All I had was water. I still cooked for my family. I read my word on a consistent basis. The church used to have a saying, "Feed your spirit and starve your flesh," which helped us to stay on task with our fast. I went twenty-one days on this fast, and I found out a lot of stuff about myself spiritually. I wondered why this fast was so easy for me. It was only hard for the first three days. After that, I was good. God brought back my memory of some things that I had forgotten about when I was a little girl.

My fast was easy because I was called to do this work. I was reminded of the time I went to school hungry and fainted in the school cafeteria, and I had the encounter with God. I cried like a baby because I had forgotten about that. Every time I needed God to change the ugly parts of me, I would go on a fast. I never did the twenty-one days again, but I had to fast on a regular basis. Fasting and prayer became a lifestyle for me.

My new lifestyle was prayer and giving my burdens to God. At night before going to sleep, I would pray and write. This happened every night until it became a habit for me. This is the stuff people don't see us believers doing. They assume we grow overnight. But that is not how it works. We must put in our time with God. I made myself available to God and became a willing vessel for him to use and to get prayers through. When I would see stuff that I didn't understand, I would just write them down.

Once I got rid of all the heaviness, what I'm supposed to be doing and where I'm supposed to be going in life became clear to me. I knew I was an author a while back, but I thought it was going to come out a different way.

One year the church was on another corporate fast, and something changed for me. I quickly found out that the purpose of my fast was to let go of some things. I believe we were in the middle of the fast, and I received a breakthrough before everyone else did. It was Wednesday 01/20/10, I remembered the date because I journaled about it. I didn't go to bible study, instead I stayed home because of the kids. Denny, my husband at the time, and I took turns. The kids had to wake up the next morning and they needed their sleep. They were usually too tired from going during the week, so I didn't take them on Wednesdays.

Anyway, when my Denny got back from church I got upset at him for some reason and immediately was disappointed. I was ready to throw him away like I did everyone else that made me mad. Then I asked God "why do I act like this," and the Holy Spirit begin to deal with me. And I heard you're not healed yet and because everyone threw you away as a child, you throw everyone away in your life. You even threw yourself away, you left yourself back in that closet all those years ago. As I laid in the bed on my back the Holy Spirit took me on a journey. I had me go all the way back in my mind to that very same closet where I lived in The Algonquin Apartments.

I visualized in my mind like a movie scene, I saw myself walking up the stairs through the apartment. As I looked side to side I remembered where everything was. I went to the room I lived in and opened the door to the closet. I begin to dig myself from under all those clothes where I use to hide. I said to myself, "it's okay you can come out now these people will not hurt you." I had to let go of all the abuse, let go of the people that shamed me, the pity, the lesbianism that taunted my mind, the incest, the anger, the rage and the past. Then I could see God giving me back everything that was locked up in that closet, where I'd left it all those years ago. I had to take back my identity, my self-esteem, and my life. It was kind of surreal for me. This freaked me out at first. But then, I realized that it was God, so I was okay. When unusual things happened to me like this, I always said, "God, if this is not You, then take it away from me in Jesus name."

The Holy Spirit reminded me of Matthew 9:17, where you can't put new wine in old wineskins. So, I let my freedom set in and thought, wow what a God. And those very people that the Holy Spirit said would not hurt me, I saw myself walking around the table praying for each and every one of them. The next Sunday was our leadership class so I gave a praise report and let everyone know what God had done for me during the fast.

I stated I have fasted many of times but this one was the hardest, as far as my body and my mind it was still going through the manifestation of the deliverance and healing. I believe that is the day people at the church started looking at me sideways. They realized I wasn't just playing; God was changing me for real. I was so excited about it, but I noticed some people looking at me crazy. I knew then they weren't experiencing anything like I was. Then I began to wonder if they were really fasting. I know I wasn't the only one that was supposed to get a breakthrough or was I? I just kept right on doing what I knew to do.

There was another shift in my life. It happened when I was asked to be head of the prayer team. I prayed about it, and I heard, "Just make yourself available." I agreed to do it, even though I didn't know what I was doing. I tried anyway.

Prayer was on Fridays. I wouldn't eat anything, even at work, after eight p.m. on Thursdays. It was hard explaining to people that I was fasting. Most of them weren't believers in Christ. I explained to them what it was and what it meant to consecrate themselves. Some knew because of lent but not about the complete fast. Leading intercessory prayer was so hard for me because I didn't get it, and there was no one really to explain it to me. I had to read books about it, but that didn't make up for the experience that I needed from someone who had already done it. I didn't have that, so I just followed the leading of the Holy Spirit. It was not always the same. Sometimes we would just worship, sometimes we would pray, and other times I just spoke in tongues until the Holy Spirit led us into what to do.

My kids were there praying with me. Sometimes they were the only support I had. I led prayer for a few years; I had to show up when no one else was there. If I were given a list of specifics to pray, I would do that. It happened more often than not that I was the only one to show up. I prayed for the leaders and I prayed for those around me. I covered a whole church until I got burned out. There were a few agreement partners, but none of them stuck in there like I did. The funny thing is, I wouldn't change anything about it. Because now I'm a friend of God, and that's the best thing that could have happened to me. Leading prayer helped build my relationship with God, and no one can take that away from me.

In those few years that I led prayer, I became so in tune with God that I would hear prayers all the time. I thought I was going to lose my mind. I had people around me who were still in sin and lying to me. That didn't help me at all, and I wanted it to stop. It was like the movie "Bruce Almighty" when the prayers were coming non-stop. That's how my mind was hearing the prayers of other people. One particular Sunday, I was on my way to the women's fellowship we had early before Sunday service begin. I was struggling so badly with all the prayers and the lies going on in my mind. The leader of the women's fellowship stopped what they were doing to pray for me once I arrived at church. Because it was so heavy on me. I thought I was going crazy.

One of the ladies by the name of Macy would always ask me, "If you're praying for everyone else, who is praying for you?"

I said I didn't know, and I hoped somebody was. Macy said, "I will be praying for you." I told her please do, because I need it. That was the hard part for me, allowing someone to help me. I was so used to being the strong one. When I'm in survival mode, that's all I know to do, just keep fighting and stay alive.

I still don't think people understand how an intercessor's mind works. It took me years to understand, and I'm still learning. I just try my best to make sure it's all about Christ. If it isn't about Christ, I don't want anything to do with it because intercession can lead us into other stuff. These are just a few ways I've had to make myself available to God. I didn't care what I had to do. I just wanted what was on me off of me. I just wanted the memory of everything I went through to go away. I just wanted to be free from the bondage of my past. Even if it meant praying for people I didn't like and who didn't like me. I had to go and apologize to people who hurt me and say, "I forgive you." Doing that caused me to let the people go.

Learning forgiveness was an important part of my process. The analogy I use is this: Consider I'm in a fight and I have someone by the neck in a head lock. I take them everywhere I go because I have them by the neck under my arms. If I go to a job interview, I have them with me. Imagine walking down the aisle to my wedding, and I still have one of these people with me in a head lock. This is what it looks like when I don't forgive and let people go for what they have done to me. I believe we hold on so long because it gives us some sense of control because we lost it when they hurt us. In the end, we look crazy because they have gone on with their lives and really believe they have never done anything, ever. So, the best thing to do is to just let go. God will handle everything. He done it for me.

Part of my healing process was to tell my family again about what happened to me as a kid. They responded indifferently. I had to tell Kam, "I am not my mom. My name is Dorothy, and I should be treated as such." She said in a sarcastic manner, "okay." That was it.

I did get one of them to ask if I wanted to confront the abusers. I said, "Nope, I'm good. God will handle every one of them." That was the conversation. They never asked if I was okay, or how was I doing with it. And to their credit, they probably didn't want the other one to know they also participated in the abuse. So, if they can stay away from the subject, they will. It probably wouldn't be a good idea anyway because I have killed everyone in my mind multiple times and multiple ways. I had to let everyone out of the head lock I had them in, in my head, and give them over to God to be dealt with. The one thing I took away from telling them, was neither one of them acted surprised. There was no compassion either. But at least they finally listened to me.

Another part of my healing process was to take a break from leading prayer. I went to see a counselor who encouraged me to go to group sessions. It helped to be around other people who understood. It helped to talk to someone who didn't know me and wouldn't judge me based on what I'd done in my past. This was a stepping stone for me to help make the pain go away. I had to make this decision for myself because there was no one around me to help me with it. I'm glad I went for myself and no one else. Most African Americans are too afraid to go to counseling. This is why the culture is still full of secrets. People are still in pain and can't get past the hurt. Go to counseling, it does help give one a voice. It doesn't matter the situation, it could be relationship issues or emotional issues, go to counseling. Having another person see things differently helps a lot. I wouldn't change anything about getting to know Christ for myself. I still believe in the church and that we will get it together eventually.

The part about my process that hurt me was feeling like I was being shunned by the very people whom I prayed for. All because I was not doing the things they were doing. After a while, I got tired of feeling alone and fighting by myself. I decided to party with them, so I went out dancing and had drinks like they did. We were like rebellious children but in the church. Acting out like our parents weren't showing us any attention. The only thing I regret about that is, I allowed myself to act like other people to fit in. If I were sound in my identity, I probably wouldn't have done it like that. So, yes, there are some things I would change, but not too much. I appreciate every experience and the lessons life has taught me. I understand that my past has gotten me to this point in my life today.

I'm so broken right now; the alabaster box has been broken open for the oil to flow in my life. The way I believe right now is not the same as how I believed a year ago. My faith is now at an all-time high; this is because I'm right where God wants me to be. Dependent on Him and trusting that He has me in His hands. God, you have my full attention. I am at Your mercy. I beckon You to my heart. Take me as I am, mold me, and shape me into Your image and Your likeness. I am Yours.

IN CLOSING

I just want to clarify to the world that my mom was an amazing woman when she was not on drugs and alcohol. She would cook and clean, and she would even listen, too. The one good thing I remember about my mom is that she loved us. Even if she didn't remember, she did. She just lost her way and could never get back on track. It didn't help that she had nothing but men around her using her every chance they got. There's one thing my mom did for me that I will never forget; she taught me how to be strong. I am a strong woman because of her. I saw how much she had to endure at the hands of others. I will admit, there are things that kids shouldn't see, but that is my reality, and I can't change it.

The best gift my mom gave me was making me a dollhouse. We lived in the Algonquin Apartments. We didn't have much money, but she blessed my soul with it. She took a cardboard box, cut out windows and doors, and even created furniture and beds. She shaped them into what they needed to be. Mom cut out pictures from a magazine and pasted them to the windows, doors, and furniture. I also had curtains and sheets for the beds. It was so creative and amazing. I thought my mom was the best for doing that for me. I had to be about eight or nine years old when she made it. I lost it when we were evicted, and I know I will never forget it.

If you don't get anything from this book, remember that God loves you and if you lose your way, always look to God for direction. God gave instructions in the Bible - the way for us to live is in there. God has not left us nor forsaken us. To be honest, we have left him. We only take what is fitting for us and use that one Scripture for everything or to show people we believe, and this is not the end.

There is more to God than just the Scripture; it's a lifestyle. There is power in His word. If we ask God who we are in Him and wait for an answer, He will reveal. He put us here on the earth for a reason, it's never too late to seek out our purpose, and everything else will follow. Help someone else along the way and do not judge people because of where they come from. We, as Christians, are the worse. We judge people by how they look.

We never know what's in people once they're cleaned up from all their baggage. If they can't find refuge in God and the people who serve Him, where else is there to go? Back into the world that they're running from? This is my truth, and I'm sticking to it, nothing more and nothing less.

ACKNOWLEDGEMENTS

Scriptures from the New American Standard Bible (NASB)

Page 9, Luke 8:17; Page 150 Isaiah 48:17;

Page 182, Matthew 9:17 Nor do people put new wine into old wineskins; otherwise the wineskins burst, and the wine pours out and the wineskins are ruined; but they put new wine into fresh wineskins, and both are preserved.

Scriptures from The New King James Bible (NKJV)

Page 34, Romans 1:4 and declared to be the Son of God with power according to the spirit of holiness, by the resurrection from the dead.

Page 75, James 1:27; Page 104, Ecclesiastes 7:17; Page 104, Deuteronomy 30:19; Page 104, Psalm 147:3; Page 106, James 1:2-4; Page 106, Ephesians 6:10-18; Page 117 John 10:10; Page 137, Isaiah 53:5;

Scriptures from The English Standard Version (ESV)

Page 27, Daniel 6:16-23 Then the king commanded, and Daniel was brought and cast in the den of lions. The King declared to Daniel, "May your God, whom you serve continually, deliver you!" 17And a stone was brought and laid on the mouth of the den, and the king sealed it with his own signet and the signet of his lords, that nothing might be changed concerning Daniel. 18Then the king went to his palace and spent the night fasting; no diversions were brought to him, and sleep fled from him. 19Then, at break of day, the king arose and went in haste to the den of lions. 20As he came near to the den where Daniel was, he cried out in a tone of anguish. The king declared to Daniel, "O Daniel, servant of the living God, has your God, whom you serve continually, been able to deliver you from the lions?" 21Then Daniel said to the king, "O king, live forever! 22My God sent his angel and shut the lions' mouths, and they have not harmed me, because I was found blameless before him; and also before you, O king, I have done no harm." 23Then the king was exceedingly glad, and commanded that Daniel be taken up out of the den. So Daniel was taken up out of the den, and no kind of harm was found on him, because he had trusted in his God.

Page 28, 2 Corinthians 10:4; Page 150, Psalm 112:1-3;

Scriptures from The New Living Translation (NLT)

Page 102, *2 Corinthians 8:9 You know the generous grace of our Lord Jesus Christ. Though he was rich, yet for your sake he became poor, so that by his poverty he could make you rich.*

Page 106, *James 1:12; Page 117, Romans 8:38-39;*

Scriptures from The New International Version (NIV)

Page 11, John 8:7; Hebrews 13:4; Romans 1:26-28; Page 12 Jude 1:7; Page 68, Deuteronomy 23:17;

Scriptures from The King James Version (KJV)

Page 13, John 10:4-5 And when he putteth forth his own sheep, he goeth before them, and the sheep follow him: for they know his voice. And a stranger will they not follow, but will flee from him: for they know not the voice of strangers.

Page 68, Romans 12:1 I beseech you therefore, brethren, by the mercies of God, that ye present your bodies a living sacrifice, holy, acceptable unto God, which is your reasonable service.

Page 90, Proverbs 29:18; Page 101, 2 Corinthians 10:4-5;

Prayers are from John Eckhardt's "Prayers that Rout Demons"

Nicole Allen for "*Proofreading Services*"

Barbara Joe Williams of Amani Publishing for "*Editing Services*"